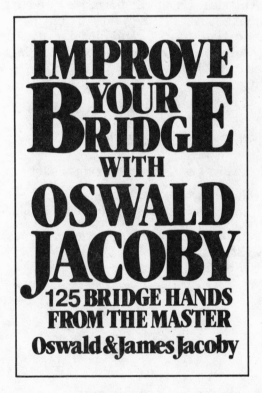

IMPROVE YOUR BRIDGE

WITH

OSWALD JACOBY

125 BRIDGE HANDS FROM THE MASTER

Oswald & James Jacoby

McGraw-Hill Book Company

New York   St. Louis   San Francisco   Auckland   Bogotá
Guatemala   Hamburg   Johannesburg   Lisbon   London   Madrid
Mexico   Montreal   New Delhi   Panama   Paris   San Juan
São Paulo   Singapore   Sydney   Tokyo   Toronto

1 2 3 4 5 6 7 8 9 F G R F G R 8 7 6 5 4 3

ISBN 0-07-032238-4

LIBRARY OF CONGRESS CATALOGING IN PUBLICATION DATA

Jacoby, Oswald, 1902–
   Improve your bridge with Oswald Jacoby.

   1. Contract bridge. I. Jacoby, James. II. Title.
GV1282.3.J243 1983   795.41'53   83-1013
ISBN 0-07-032238-4

Book design by Carol Waters

Contents

1 Bidding

There are certain basic principles of bidding that should be assumed by anyone who wants to enjoy bridge without making it his or her sole interest in life. The bidding is what is generally known as standard American. This is the best system for anyone; don't let the system mongers who come up with various artificial systems fool you. Standard American works and is the simplest base for bidding.

It is the first effective system. In the early days of contract bridge, most of it came from Culbertson, Sims, Lightner, Zedwitz, Schenken, and Jacoby. Goren, who appeared on the scene later, added much, as other players have from time to time.

Point count was first used by Jacoby and later popularized by Goren and Fred Karpin. Today every good player uses the 4-3-2-1 count. The following table shows the elements of point count usage:

High-Card Points

Each ace . . . . 4 points
Each king . . . . 3 points
Each queen . . . . 2 points
Each jack . . . . 1 point

Distributional Points

(a) Each void (blank suit) . . . . 3 points
Each singleton (one-card suit) . . . . 2 points
Each doubleton (two-card suit) . . . . 1 point
(b) Add one point for each card over four in any suit
that is so strong you do not need partner's support
to establish it.
(c) SUBTRACT one point for 4-3-3-3 distribution.
THIS IS MOST IMPORTANT.
(d) Count distributional points for suit bids only.

Key Numbers to Remember

Grand slam (all 13 tricks). . . . . 37 points
Small slam (12 tricks) . . . . 33 points
Minor suit game (11 tricks) . . . . 29 points
Major suit game (10 tricks). . . . . 26 points
Notrump game (9 tricks). . . . . 26 points

Points do not take tricks, cards do. You do not
bid in a vacuum. In competitive situations you
must realize that some points will become worthless. Others may even increase in value.

In valuing a hand, bear in mind that tens and
nines give your hand body. Point count cards become more valuable when supported by lower

cards. Unsupported honors go down in value. Thus, in hand valuation it is good general policy to count one distributional point, not two, for a singleton honor, even an ace, and to add no distributional point at all for doubleton honors.

Basic Bidding Principles

The first and most important principle is that each bid or pass places a top and bottom limit on your strength. Subsequent action tends to define your limits more closely, but never increases them.

The second principle is preparedness. When you have choice of action you should choose the one that is most likely to make future action simpler.

The third is that of risk versus action. Before you take any action, balance the risk of loss against the prospect of gain.

The opening bid is the cornerstone of both attack and defense. There are all sorts of guidelines here, but we will try to give the simplest possible set, temporarily omitting preemptive openings based on a long suit, a stout heart, and a desire to make things difficult for your opponents who presumably have more high cards than you.

The first requirement is high-card points, which we will call HCP from now on. Here are the minimum standards:

14 HCP or more   Always open bidding
13 HCP   95 percent of hands should be opened
12 HCP   75 percent should be opened
11 HCP   25 percent should be opened
10 HCP   Do not open

There is a lot of balderdash about the weaker standards in third or fourth seat. Your bridge life will be sweeter and easier if you just consider that if a hand is worth an opening bid it is worth it in any position.

The fact that a hand meets all requirements for an opening bid does not mean that you must bid with it after an opponent has opened the bidding.

One Notrump Opening Hand

In the first days of contract, the notrump bid was a sort of football to be kicked around by writers. Culbertson used a different notrump every year. Sims used a strong notrump. No one knew just how strong, but it varied from what would be a modern 18 HCP up to 23 or 24. Lenz used a weak notrump. And so on, ad infinitum.

It remained for Oswald Jacoby, who was trying to teach his tennis-playing wife the game of bridge, to introduce a point-count notrump that has been practically unchanged since 1932. Maybe that notrump has real permanency. 1983 will mark the Jacobys' fifty-first wedding anniversary, and Mrs. J still claims that her husband tends to cheat and open 15-point notrumps when he plays with her. Mr. J claims that the husband still has the right to bid most of the notrumps (women's lib to the contrary) and has the overtricks to prove it.

Seriously, the standard notrump is 16-18 HCP but nearly all experts reduce the limits to 15-17. Take your pick, but do not, repeat do not, use 15-18. All notrump openings should be precise bids and if you have too wide a high-card margin, you lose too much precision.

The opening notrump should show a balanced hand with one of these three patterns: 4-3-3-3, 4-4-3-2, or 5-3-3-2. This has been standard since 1932, but there has been one change. In 1932 we required that if there were a doubleton, it had to include one of the three top honors. Today we bid it with the jack and lots of players open notrump with any doubleton at all.

Don't fall too much in love with notrump openings. In particular, don't bid a 19-point notrump. More important, don't ever open notrump with a singleton. Such hands are so likely to play better in a suit that you want to start with a suit bid.

Finally, when your partner opens notrump tend to prefer a final notrump game contract to an 11-trick minor suit game.

Opening One of a Suit

This is your workhorse bid. It can be made with any distribution and almost any high-card strength.

You don't open one of a suit when your hand meets all requirements for a bid in notrump or is strong enough so you can afford to open with a strong forcing bid. At the minimum end of the spectrum you normally require at least 11 HCP (one point more than your fair share of high cards).

With that 11 HCP you open only when you have a six-card suit or a good five-card suit and not always then.

With 12 HCP, pass with 4-3-3-3 and open most of the time with any other distribution.

With 13 HCP you are a full king above average. You should pass only with 4-3-3-3 distribution and very seldom then.

Get up to 14 HCP and you have the equivalent of an ace above average. You can't afford not to open.

Choice of a Suit

When you have a two-suiter (two suits of five cards or more), you open the higher ranking if they are equal in length and the longer if they are unequal. With just one five-card suit, you open that suit. With no five-card suit you always have a choice.

Suppose you pick up: S- A Q x x   H- K x x   D- J x x   C- A x x. In the early days of contract this hand presented no problem. You opened one spade with your good four-card spade suit. Somehow or other even those early players found this start led to trouble. You got all sorts of bad game contracts. Around 1932 the young experts of that day started opening these hands with one club and the three-card club opening had arrived.

Not that this club bid is not forcing. If you use it regularly you can expect to be left in it once every couple of years. You can expect to find yourself raised to two or three considerably more often, but in such circumstances your partner is going to have at least four clubs to help you.

Jacoby Transfer Bids

The basic Jacoby transfer bid, which we will call JTB, uses two-diamond and two-heart responses to an opening notrump as artificial forcing bids that show the next higher suit.

Thus, two diamonds shows at least five hearts and asks opener to bid two hearts; two hearts shows five spades and asks opener to bid two spades.

After the opener responds to show the transfer, the next bid shows more about the hand.

Take a hand like: S- Q J x x x x H- x x D- x x x C- x x. Your partner opens one notrump. You want the hand to play in two spades. If you aren't playing JTB you bid two spades. If everything goes well, you play it there and the opening lead is right through your partner's strength and may well cost you a trick. Playing JTB your partner plays two spades and gets the advantage of the lead up to him.

Make your hand a trifle better by changing hearts to A x. You raise two spades to three after your partner replies to the transfer. You have invited game and the play will be in the right hand. Now make the hearts A K. You just raise his two spades to four.

Suppose you hold: S- Q J x x H- A x D- Q x x C- x x x opposite partner's notrump. Bid the two-hearts transfer and then bid two notrump over opener's two spades. This lets him pass, bid three notrump, three spades, or four spades depending on his hand.

Make your hand a trifle better, such as S- Q J x
x x   H- A x   D- Q J x   C- 10 x x, and your rebid
is three notrump to let him choose between three
notrump or four spades as the final contract.

Proper Common Sense Bids

The bidding methods discussed are not simple,
but they are all common sensical and worth learning.

We try to avoid four-card major-suit openings
and will open any three-card club suit or three-
card diamond suit if it includes one of the three
top honors in preference to a four-card major.

In responding at the two level we try to have at
least an 11-point hand and consider the bid as
being almost a game force.

We promise to rebid if opener has bid anything
except two of his own suit and opener promises to
keep on bidding unless our second bid is just three
of our own suit.

Thus, 1S-2D-2S may be passed by a responder,
but is not likely to be.

Any simple rebid after a two-over-one response
may be made with a minimum hand and does not
guarantee any extra values.

It is up to the next bid to show them. Here are
some partnership sequences:

1. 1S-2D-2H-3D-3S. Opener probably has
something like S- A Q 10 9 6 5   H- A J 7 6   D- Q
3   C- 2 or maybe a trifle better.

2. 1D-2C-2S-2NT-3NT. Opener may have as
little as S- A K x x   H- x x x   D- A Q x x   C- x x.
He should not have much more.

Finally, we are going to give you an added complication which you may want to use with regular partners. When you respond two hearts to a one-spade opening you promise either real spade support or a five-card heart suit; and, you promise a rebid even if he just bids two spades.

Basic Bidding Rules Recap

Using the standard American bidding system you can add as many gadgets as you wish. Just bear in mind that a gadget is fine as long as you and your partner don't forget it or let it confuse you.

We recommend these basic rules for bidding:

1. Always open the bidding with 14 HCP, nearly always with 13, often with 12, and occasionally with 11. Remember that the strength for an opening bid does not always justify getting in against an adverse opening.

2. The one-notrump opening should show 16-18 or 15-17 HCP, but not 15-18.

3. Use Blackwood and Stayman.

4. Tend to overbid with good hands and under-bid with bad ones.

5. Make sure that you and your partners work together. Remember that if your partner loses you do also.

Suggestions for slightly advanced bidding:

1. Use weak two bids with two clubs as the only forcing opening.

2. Use the Jacoby transfer in one of its simpler forms.

It doesn't require much study to use one or both of these conventions that are almost as common in tournament play as Blackwood and Stayman.

Explaining the "limit" raise

```
                NORTH
                ♠ 10 6 2
                ♥ K 8 7 3
                ♦ Q J 9 5
                ♣ A J
WEST                      EAST
♠ K J 9 5 3              ♠ A Q 7 4
♥ 9                      ♥ 10 5 2
♦ 10 8 7 3 2            ♦ A
♣ 4 2                    ♣ K 10 7 5 3
                SOUTH
                ♠ 8
                ♥ A Q J 6 4
                ♦ K 6 4
                ♣ Q 9 8 6
```

Vulnerable: East-West
Dealer: South

West	North	East	South
			1♥
Pass	3♥	Pass	4♥
Pass	Pass	Pass	

Opening lead:♦3

In one sense any time you · raise your partner's suit you are making a limit bid. The term is not necessary when referring to such bids as a single raise or a raise to game. Everyone knows that the player who makes such a bid is placing definite close limits to both his minimum and maximum strength.

Now, assume your partner opens one heart and you jump to three hearts. In basic standard American you are making a game forcing bid. You say "Partner, you must bid again."

In the last 30 years, advanced standard American bidders do not play that bid as a force, but do play it as strongly invitational.

Today's North hand is a good example of this limit jump raise. He has a good hand, but not enough for game. South does go to game because in general when you hold a singleton your hand possesses good offensive possibilities.

West opens a diamond. East takes his ace and plays the ace of spades. Had he underled it, West would be able to give him a ruff and the king of clubs would produce the setting trick. As it is South makes the game.

Not playing limit raises, North would respond two diamonds. East might well try a takeout double with both other suits and a good opening bid. If he did East-West would probably play and make four spades, but the limit raise had shut them out.

Deft drop dumps declarer

```
            NORTH
            ♠ A 10 5
            ♥ K 7 6
            ♦ A K 10 3
            ♣ K J 6
WEST                    EAST
♠ Q J 7 6              ♠ K 3
♥ 5 2                  ♥ A Q 4
♦ 9 7 4               ♦ 8 5 2
♣ 8 5 4 3            ♣ Q 10 9 7 2
            SOUTH
            ♠ 9 8 4 2
            ♥ J 10 9 8 3
            ♦ Q J 6
            ♣ A
```

Vulnerable: Neither
Dealer: West

West	North	East	South
Pass	1 ♦	Pass	1 ♥
Pass	2 NT	Pass	3 ♦
Pass	3 ♥	Pass	4 ♥
Pass	Pass	Pass	

Opening lead: ♠ Q

North and South were using a 15-17 point notrump, which explains why North opened one club and jumped to two notrump over the heart reponse.

South's three-diamond call was normal, as was North's three hearts. At this point South might well have tried three notrump instead of four hearts. Three notrump would have waltzed home and four hearts might have made, but South went wrong at trick one and gave East a chance to make the killing defensive play.

West's spade lead gave the defense its only chance. If South had ducked that queen he would have made the game. But he decided that maybe there was a 5-1 spade break against him, so South clattered up with dummy's ace.

Now it was East's turn to think. If he followed small to the ace, as most players would automatically do, South would still make his heart game. He would come to one spade trick, three hearts, four diamonds and two clubs.

East knew his side had three tricks: one spade and two trump. If West held the jack of spades, as his lead indicated, there was a way, East realized, of scoring three trump tricks and one spade trick.

Consequently, East dropped his king on the ace of spades and now declarer could no longer make his game. When East won the first heart with his queen, he returned a spade to West's jack and ruffed the spade return. The ace of trump was the defense's fourth trick.

Careful play wins

```
              NORTH
              ♠ 10 2
              ♥ A 8 5
              ♦ K 8 6 3
              ♣ 8 6 5 4
WEST                        EAST
♠ 5                         ♠ 8 7 6 3
♥ K Q J 6 4 3               ♥ 10 9 2
♦ 10 4 2                    ♦ Q J 9 7
♣ A K J                     ♣ Q 10
              SOUTH
              ♠ A K Q J 9 4
              ♥ 7
              ♦ A 5
              ♣ 9 7 3 2
```

Vulnerable: East-West
Dealer: South

West	North	East	South
			1♠
2♥	Dbl.	Pass	3♠
Pass	Pass	Pass	

Opening lead: ♥K

Here is a hand from a Swiss team match at the Dallas regional. Both sides were using negative doubles so after West's two-heart overcall each North decided to double to show his seven HCP and support for both unbid suits. At table one, South jumped to three spades and North decided that he had bid more than he should have and passed.

The play was short and easy. Dummy's ace of hearts took the first trick. South played four rounds of trumps to pull East's and tried to establish a diamond. Unfortunately for him, West had discarded two diamonds and just one heart on the spades. South was held to his contract since he never got a club trick.

North and South remarked that they had been lucky to stop at three. When time came to compare it turned out that the other South had bid and made four spades by simple, but careful play.

At trick two he led a club from dummy. West won and forced him with a heart. South led a second club. Again West won and forced him, but South just led a third club. Now dummy's 10 of trumps was there to ruff another heart lead so this South was able to draw trumps and make his 10th trick with an established club.

Poor contract, good play

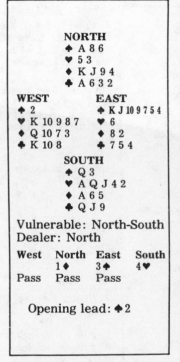

NORTH
♠ A 8 6
♥ 5 3
♦ K J 9 4
♣ A 6 3 2

WEST
♠ 2
♥ K 10 9 8 7
♦ Q 10 7 3
♣ K 10 8

EAST
♠ K J 10 9 7 5 4
♥ 6
♦ 8 2
♣ 7 5 4

SOUTH
♠ Q 3
♥ A Q J 4 2
♦ A 6 5
♣ Q J 9

Vulnerable: North-South
Dealer: North

West	North	East	South
	1♦	3♠	4♥
Pass	Pass	Pass	

Opening lead: ♠2

East's aggressive three-spade preempt successfully pushed North-South into a poor four-heart contract when three notrump would have been easy.

South groaned when he saw the dummy. A penalty double would have been better than playing a precarious game in hearts. Still, the problem was to make the contract, not linger on might-have-beens.

South won the opening spade lead with dummy's ace. He knew the spade lead was a singleton. He took a trump finesse which lost to the king.

West returned a trump, exposing the foul distribution in that suit. It almost seemed hopeless for declarer. He had three trump losers, a spade loser and minor suit finesses to negotiate. Nevertheless, through extremely skillful play (and luck), declarer was able to make the contract.

At trick four he played the queen of clubs, which was covered by the king and ace. He played a diamond to his ace, successfully finessed dummy's jack of diamonds, cashed the king, and ruffed a diamond with a low trump.

The stage was set for an unusual end-play against West. Declarer cashed his high trump and exited with his remaining low trump. West had to win and eventually had to lead a club into South's jack-nine.

Declarer had taken one spade trick, two high trumps, three diamonds, a diamond ruff with a low trump and three club tricks.

Loser on loser wins game

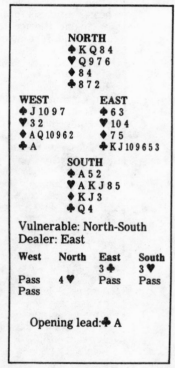

NORTH
♠ K Q 8 4
♥ Q 9 7 6
♦ 8 4
♣ 8 7 2

WEST
♠ J 10 9 7
♥ 3 2
♦ A Q 10 9 6 2
♣ A

EAST
♠ 6 3
♥ 10 4
♦ 7 5
♣ K J 10 9 6 5 3

SOUTH
♠ A 5 2
♥ A K J 8 5
♦ K J 3
♣ Q 4

Vulnerable: North-South
Dealer: East

West	North	East	South
		3 ♣	3 ♥
Pass	4 ♥	Pass	Pass
Pass			

Opening lead:♣ A

Pre-emptive bids can be two-edged swords. Sometimes they impede the opponents from reaching their proper contract and at other times they give declarer a valuable clue in the play.

South probably should have doubled at his first opportunity, but his three-heart overcall struck good support and was raised to game.

The opening club lead was obvious. West switched to a trump at the second trick and declarer drew two rounds with his ace and king.

South hoped for an even division in spades to accommodate his club loser. He played the ace, king and queen of spades, but they failed to split.

South thought of a new line of play. Because of the bidding and early play, West's ace of clubs had surely been a singleton.

What if he played the fourth round of spades and discarded his club loser? West would be left on play with nothing but diamonds to lead. Declarer would lose one club, one spade and only one diamond. Consequently, South led the fourth spade and pitched his club loser on his spade loser, which effectively end played West.

South "guessed" how to play diamonds by having the opponents play them for him.

Making the right grand slam

NORTH
♠ A J 10 5
♥ K
♦ K 8 5 4 3
♣ A 10 5

WEST
♠ 9 7 4 3
♥ 9 8 4 2
♦ 6
♣ J 7 4 3

EAST
♠ 6
♥ 10 7 6 5 3
♦ J 10 9 2
♣ Q 9 8

SOUTH
♠ K Q 8 2
♥ A Q J
♦ A Q 7
♣ K 6 2

Vulnerable: East-West
Dealer: South

West	North	East	South
			1♣
Pass	1♦	Pass	2♣
Pass	3♣	Pass	4♣
Pass	5♣	Pass	5♦
Pass	6♣	Pass	7♣
Pass	Pass	Pass	

Opening lead: ♠3

Seven no trump is a pretty good contract with the North-South cards. All declarer requires is a 3-2 diamond break and even if diamonds don't break there is a slight extra chance. If the player with four diamonds is the only one who can stop clubs he will be squeezed.

Diamonds don't break and the squeeze isn't there so that any North-South pair that bid seven no trump was down one for a bad score. Even in the Life Masters' Pairs only a quarter of the field reached seven and most of those in seven were in spades.

The bidding in the box is instructive. South's club opening on a three card suit is normal in standard American. He is too strong for one no trump and too weak for two. After that start the bidding could proceed in any number of ways, but we like that shown in the box.

South won the spade with his eight and led the deuce to dummy's 10. Then he stopped to see the best way to guard against a 4-1 diamond break. He cashed dummy's ace of clubs and his three hearts while discarding two clubs from dummy. Then he ruffed his last low club with the ace of trumps, drew trumps and claimed.

The club ruff had been his 13th winner.

Poor play hurts

```
                NORTH
                ♠ 8
                ♥ K 3 2
                ♦ K Q J 10 8 5 4 2
                ♣ 9
WEST                      EAST
♠ 10 4 3                  ♠ J 9 7 6 2
♥ Q J 9                   ♥ A 10 6
♦ 7 6 3                   ♦ 9
♣ 7 5 4 3                 ♣ J 10 8 6
                SOUTH
                ♠ A K Q 5
                ♥ 8 7 5 4
                ♦ A
                ♣ A K Q 2
```

Vulnerable: North-South
Dealer: West

West	North	East	South
Pass	3♦	Pass	3 NT
Pass	Pass	Pass	

Opening lead: ♥Q

North's vulnerable three diamond preempt with an eight-card suit and an outside king would not be made by most experts. The modern tendency among experts in making vulnerable three level preempts is to have a good seven card suit with little outside strength. North deviated by having too much side strength and that eight diamond.

South had no idea what to bid over North's preempt. Although North is cold for six diamonds from his position, it is hard to judge. Anyhow, South tried three no trump. If North had three small hearts and a black jack, three no trump could be the only makeable game.

North proudly displayed his dummy, commenting that this was the strongest three diamond bid he had ever made. Unfortunately, after a heart lead through his king, declarer could manage only eight tricks. Not one of those was taken by North's "magnificent" dummy. "Perhaps," lamented South, "Your hand wasn't so good."

Both North and South have asked us to assess the blame for this disaster. We charge South 25 percent. He should not try three no trump with that singleton ace of diamonds, but we give North the other 75 percent.

As North said, he had a super strength preempt. He should have passed or opened four diamonds, but over South's three no trump North should have gone back to diamonds. Had he jumped to five South might have bid the slam.

2 ARCH

Some 10 years ago, Oswald Jacoby devised the acronym "ARCH" as a reminder of what you should do at trick one.

A—Analyze the lead. As declarer this should enable you to get some immediate idea of how the 25 cards you aren't looking at are likely to be divided.

R—Review the bidding. If your opponents have bid, work out what their bids meant. If they haven't bid you may also be able to get ideas.

C—Count winners and losers. Check on which tricks are surely yours and which tricks are surely theirs and see what you can do about the doubtful ones.

H—How can I make my contract? This is the major problem. Overtricks are fine, but the nitty-gritty is the contract itself. The ARC are all guides to the final H.

As declarer, you will also have two defenders working against you. Their "H" is "How can I defeat this contract?" and they will be using every legitimate play at their disposal to upset your applecart.

There are certain standard defensive plays starting with conventions that apply to leads, signals, etc. This is a major guide to the defenders and almost as helpful to declarer. As declarer you ask yourself why that particular suit was led and why that particular card was selected.

It is sometimes like the old story of how a stray horse was found. The expert said, "I just ask myself where I would go if I were a horse."

We want to mention that ARCH is based on ARC devised by George Gooden of California, for many years one of this country's finest and most distinguished bridge teachers.

ARCH at work

```
                    NORTH
                ♠ A J 10
                ♥ A 4
                ♦ J 10 9 4
                ♣ K Q 6 4
WEST                          EAST
♠ 7 6 3                       ♠ 9 8 5 2
♥ K J 7 5 2                   ♥ 10 6
♦ A 5 2                       ♦ 7 6 3
♣ A 9                         ♣ 7 5 3 2
                    SOUTH
                ♠ K Q 4
                ♥ Q 9 8 3
                ♦ K Q 8
                ♣ J 10 8
```

Vulnerable: Neither
Dealer: West

West	North	East	South
1♥	Dbl.	Pass	2 NT
Pass	3 NT	Pass	Pass
Pass			

Opening lead: ♥5

South had a chance to apply all four letters of ARCH before playing to trick one.

He Analyzed the lead as fourth best from a suit headed by king - jack, or maybe king-10, but not king-jack-10.

He Reviewed the bidding and noted that West, who had opened one heart, was marked with both minor suit aces.

He Counted winners and losers and saw that he had plenty of winners if he could knock out both aces before West had time to establish three heart winners.

He asked, "How can I make my contract?"

That was quite a problem, but he finally solved it and came up with an unusual play. He went right up with dummy's ace of hearts.

He knocked out West's ace of clubs. West continued with the deuce of hearts. East played the 10 and now South was ready with the second step in his campaign. He let East hold the trick.

East could not lead a heart. He didn't have one. So East led a diamond. West took his ace and after a lot of thought cashed his king of hearts. If he hadn't done that South, would have made an overtrick.

Note that if South had let the first heart ride around to his queen West would have been able to establish three heart tricks before South could knock out both aces.

ARCH for the defense

```
              NORTH
              ♠ K Q 9 8 5
              ♥ 9 8 6
              ♦ 9 7
              ♣ K Q 10
WEST                    EAST
♠ 6 4                   ♠ 7
♥ A 7 5 3               ♥ J 10 2
♦ Q 8 3 2               ♦ A K 10 6 5 4
♣ 9 7 3                 ♣ A 8 5
              SOUTH
              ♠ A J 10 3 2
              ♥ K Q 4
              ♦ J
              ♣ J 6 4 2
```

Vulnerable: Neither
Dealer: East

West	North	East	South
		1♦	1♠
2♦	3♠	Pass	4♠
Pass	Pass	Pass	

Opening lead: ♦ 2

East took his king of diamonds and was about to continue with the ace. Then he stopped to put the acronym "ARCH" to work.

He Analyzed the lead. Third or fourth best — probably fourth best.

He Reviewed the bidding. West had raised him. West undoubtedly had something in addition to the queen of diamonds. Dummy held the clubs. Therefore, it had to be in hearts.

Then he Counted his winners. One or possibly two diamonds, plus one club, plus one or maybe two in hearts.

It seemed imperative to attack hearts right away. The second diamond was not going to run away in any event.

Which heart to lead? The standard lead from jack-10-small is the jack, but this did not seem to be the right time for the standard lead.

East led the deuce.

What should declarer do? You can see the four of hearts is the winning play, but declarer could not. He played his queen. West took his ace and led back a heart. The defense got their two heart tricks.

Note that if East tried to cash a second diamond, South would ruff, draw trumps, knock out the club ace, discard a heart from dummy on his fourth club and make his game.

Ask the Experts

You hold:
- ♠ K 2
- ♥ K 10 7 6 5
- ♦ A Q 2
- ♣ K Q 8

A Dakota reader asks if we recommend a heart or notrump opening with this hand.

We definitely recommend a one-notrump opening because if you open one heart you will be really in a quandary if partner responds either one spade or one notrump.

ARCH by the professor

NORTH
- ♠ K 10
- ♥ K 6 3
- ♦ J 5 2
- ♣ A K J 9 3

WEST
- ♠ Q 8 7 6 4
- ♥ 10 9 8 2
- ♦ A 10 8
- ♣ 2

EAST
- ♠ J 2
- ♥ 7
- ♦ K 9 7 6 4
- ♣ Q 10 8 7 5

SOUTH
- ♠ A 9 5 3
- ♥ A Q J 5 4
- ♦ Q 3
- ♣ 6 4

Vulnerable: North-South
Dealer: South

West	North	East	South
			1♥
1♠	2♣	Pass	2♥
Pass	4♥	Pass	Pass
Pass			

Opening lead: ♣2

The professor was holding forth on the use of ARCH.

He explained: "That lead was surely a singleton. West surely has five or six spades. His overcall wasn't much in any event, but this West likes to bid whether he has a bid or not."

"How can I make ten tricks? I can win that club, draw trumps, lead a spade and play dummy's ten if West plays low. West should have both queen and jack of spades, but maybe he hasn't and the hand will collapse if East captures the ten with either the queen or jack. Now I will show you a line of play that is sure to succeed as long as all five trumps aren't in one hand."

Here is the Professor's sure-thing play.

He wins the club and draws trumps while discarding one club from dummy. East's best discards will be one club and two diamonds and we assume they will be made.

Now comes the key play. South leads his second club and plays either the nine or jack while West will surely throw away a spade.

East is in with the first defensive trick and a serious headache.

A club lead is obvious suicide. A spade lead will give South three sure spade tricks and allow him to get rid of one of his diamonds on a high club.

Finally a diamond lead will make it possible for South to set up dummy's jack for one spade discard while another spade will go on a high club.

ARCH for safety

```
              NORTH
              ♠ 6
              ♥ J 5 4
              ♦ A K Q 9 3
              ♣ K 10 8 3
WEST                        EAST
♠ Q 10 5 2                  ♠ 7 4
♥ A K Q 9 6 2               ♥ 10 8 7 3
♦ 10 7                      ♦ J 6 4
♣ A                         ♣ 6 5 4 2
              SOUTH
              ♠ A K J 9 8 3
              ♥ - - - -
              ♦ 8 5 2
              ♣ Q J 9 7
```

Vulnerable: Both
Dealer: North

West	North	East	South
	1♦	Pass	1♠
2♥	Pass	Pass	4♠
Dbl.	Pass	Pass	Pass

Opening lead: ♥ K

South Analyzes the lead as from West's bid suit. A Review of the bidding indicates that West probably has exactly six hearts. With seven he might well have tried a preemptive jump to three. In any event South ruffs the heart.

South can go after six. All that requires is that he take a successful trump finesse and find the suit splitting 3-3.

South wants to make the 10 tricks he has bid for. He has to lose a club trick and can afford to lose two trump tricks.

So when he asks, "How can I make my contract?" the answer is that he should be willing to lose two trumps, but unwilling to let the defense have time to make him ruff a second heart before the ace of clubs is knocked out.

What is the safest way to keep control?

South should promptly cash the ace and king of trumps. If the suit breaks five-one he is in trouble, but as long as it breaks either 4-2 or 3-3 he is safe at home. He just knocks out the ace of clubs, ruffs the next heart and leads out clubs and diamonds. The defenders make two trump tricks, but South makes his four spade contract.

Ask the Experts

You hold:

♠ A 10 8 2
♥ K J 9 4
♦ Q
♣ K Q J 7

The bidding is opened to your right with one diamond. You make a takeout double, but everyone passes. A Washington reader asks what he should lead.

The queen of diamonds is the correct lead. You want to start getting rid of trumps. Your partner almost surely has some high cards and you sacrifice your queen in hope of eventually stopping declarer from taking tricks with small ones.

3 Playing the Hand

Finesses

Finesses are the most common bridge plays. They are attempts to score a trick with a card that is lower than one held by an opponent by taking advantage of its position in the North, East, South, West rotation. The first play a beginner must learn is the finesse. Then, after learning how to finesse he or she must learn when not to.

You don't take a finesse merely because it is there for the taking, but you should take it nearly all the time.

Finessing away a game

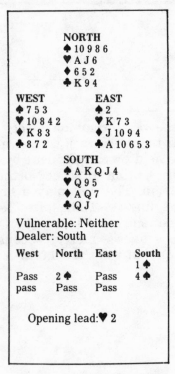

NORTH
♠ 10 9 8 6
♥ A J 6
♦ 6 5 2
♣ K 9 4

WEST
♠ 7 5 3
♥ 10 8 4 2
♦ K 8 3
♣ 8 7 2

EAST
♠ 2
♥ K 7 3
♦ J 10 9 4
♣ A 10 6 5 3

SOUTH
♠ A K Q J 4
♥ Q 9 5
♦ A Q 7
♣ Q J

Vulnerable: Neither
Dealer: South

West	North	East	South
			1 ♠
Pass	2 ♠	Pass	4 ♠
pass	Pass	Pass	

Opening lead: ♥ 2

South lost no time going down one at his four-spade contract. He played dummy's six of hearts at trick one. East took his king and led back the jack of diamonds. Now South had to lose two diamonds and the ace of clubs.

"I must have my own special cloud hanging over my head like Joe Btspflik. Finesses work for every one else, but never for me, and I am also looking at the most deadly opening lead. Etc. Etc." complained South.

"I am the real Joe Btspflik," groaned North. "I must be the most thrown partner of the year and it is only February."

North was right. South would have made a lot of tricks if West had led from the king of hearts, but he had contracted for just 10 and 10 tricks were right there for the taking if he had really wanted them. All he needed to do was to refuse the heart finesse.

Then he could cash three high trumps and lead his queen of clubs.

East could take his ace and lead back a diamond. South would finesse the queen unsuccessfully, but now would be able to get a discard of the seven of diamonds on dummy's king of clubs and would have his 10 tricks.

Make your own luck

```
              NORTH
              ♠ A Q J
              ♥ 8 3
              ♦ A Q J 9
              ♣ K Q J 3
WEST                      EAST
♠ 9 5 4 3                 ♠ 10 8 7
♥ K Q 10 9 5 4            ♥ 7 2
♦ K 6                     ♦ 8 7 4 2
♣ 5                       ♣ A 9 7 6
              SOUTH
              ♠ K 6 2
              ♥ A J 6
              ♦ 10 5 3
              ♣ 10 8 4 2
```

Vulnerable: North-South
Dealer: North

West	North	East	South
	1♦	Pass	1 NT
2♥	3♥	Pass	3 NT
Pass	Pass	Pass	

Opening lead: ♥K

The unlucky expert had cornered us again. He started out with, "I ought to quit bridge and take up some other game, but with my luck other games would probably be worse for me. Look at this hand."

He scribbled it out and continued, "I was in three no-trump, down three tricks. Anyone else would have made four or five odd."

We looked the scribble over in admiration. Not of his skill, but rather the swindle perpetrated against him by West. It was easy for us to work out since there was only one logical way for him to wind up that deep in the ashcan.

West must have opened the king of hearts. Needless to say, the U.E. let it hold. Then West carefully shifted to the six of diamonds.

A tough play to make, but quite logical if West studied all possibilities. West could see that South must hold the ace-jack of hearts and either the king of spades or the ace of clubs. Should South hold the club ace nothing could hurt him. But look what did happen when East held that important card.

South didn't dare try a diamond finesse. He had to assume that West held the ace of clubs. So South took dummy's ace of diamonds and played a club. East took his ace and cleared hearts for his partner.

Now our unfortunate friend led a diamond. West cashed the diamond king and four hearts for down three.

Unlucky indeed, but normal for our friend.

Because it was there

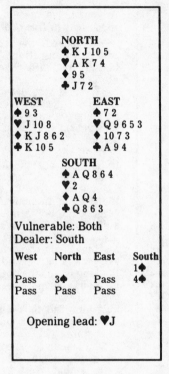

NORTH
♠ K J 10 5
♥ A K 7 4
♦ 9 5
♣ J 7 2

WEST
♠ 9 3
♥ J 10 8
♦ K J 8 6 2
♣ K 10 5

EAST
♠ 7 2
♥ Q 9 6 5 3
♦ 10 7 3
♣ A 9 4

SOUTH
♠ A Q 8 6 4
♥ 2
♦ A Q 4
♣ Q 8 6 3

Vulnerable: Both
Dealer: South

West	North	East	South
			1♠
Pass	3♠	Pass	4♠
Pass	Pass	Pass	

Opening lead: ♥J

"Why did you take the diamond finesse?" asked North.

"Because it was there for the taking," replied South. "If it had worked I would have made my game."

South had lost the diamond finesse and while he had been able to discard one of his clubs on a good heart he had been forced to start the club suit himself and since each defender held three clubs to a top honor the defense collected three club tricks.

With trumps breaking 2-2, South really had no reason to take that diamond finesse. He should win the first heart as he did, ruff a heart high and draw trumps with two leads. Then he could discard his four or even his queen of diamonds on the king of hearts, ruff dummy's last heart and play ace and another diamond.

Then South could claim his contract. A heart or diamond lead would let South ruff with his last trump and discard one of dummy's clubs. A club lead would give South an automatic club trick.

As North said to South later on, "Too bad you were dealt the diamond queen."

Good day or bad day?

```
                NORTH
                ♠ A 8 5 3
                ♥ 6 4
                ♦ A J 8 2
                ♣ Q J 6
WEST                        EAST
♠ J 9 4 2                   ♠ Q 10
♥ K Q J 10 8                ♥ 7 3 2
♦ 4                         ♦ K 5 3
♣ K 9 7                     ♣ 8 5 4 3 2
                SOUTH
                ♠ K 7 6
                ♥ A 9 5
                ♦ Q 10 9 7 6
                ♣ A 10
```

Vulnerable: Both
Dealer: East

West	North	East	South
		Pass	1♦
1♥	1♠	Pass	1 NT
Pass	2♦	Pass	3 NT

Opening lead: ♥K

If an expert expects a finesse to lose, he will still take it if no other play will work, but he sure looks around to find that other play first. On a good day South will find the king of diamonds to his left and make a lot of no-trump. Today isn't a good one.

South ducks two hearts but wins the third one. Then he loses the diamond finesse to East and a club comes back.

Good day or bad day, South does not expect that the club finesse will succeed. Is there any play to make his contract if West holds the king of clubs?

The answer is a resounding "yes."

If West holds four or five spades, the diamond suit will squeeze him out of either his spade guard or the king of clubs or force him to throw all his hearts.

South takes his ace of clubs and runs the diamonds. West must make four discards. The first three are easy. One club, one spade and one heart. The fourth is impossible.

If West discards his last heart, South simply leads his 10 of clubs and sets up a club trick in dummy. If he throws the king of clubs, South makes an overtrick. If he chucks another spade, declarer makes three spade tricks. Bad day or not, South has made his game.

Trump policeman does job

NORTH
- ♠ 7 5 4
- ♥ J 9
- ♦ 7 4 3
- ♣ K 9 6 3 2

WEST
- ♠ K Q J 6
- ♥ 8 5 4 2
- ♦ Q 9 5 2
- ♣ 8

EAST
- ♠ A 10 9 3
- ♥ 7 3
- ♦ 8 6
- ♣ Q J 10 7 5

SOUTH
- ♠ 8 2
- ♥ A K Q 10 6
- ♦ A K J 10
- ♣ A 4

Vulnerable: East-West
Dealer: South

West	North	East	South
			2♥
Pass	2 NT	Pass	3♦
Pass	3♥	Pass	4♥
Pass	Pass	Pass	

Opening lead: ♠K

South gets to four hearts on account of the honors and his good hand.

He ruffs the third spade and sees that a successful diamond finesse will let him make an overtrick unless trumps break 5-1.

How about an unsuccess-ful diamond finesse? He will still make four if trumps break 3-3. Can he handle a 4-2 trump break and losing diamond finesse?

Yes, he can if he puts a trump policeman to work.

South ruffs the third spade. Leads his 10 of trumps to dummy's jack, takes and loses the diamond finesse.

West had the third defensive trick and would like to lead his last spade and force South to ruff, but there is that policeman trump in dummy ready to ruff a spade and protect declarer.

West can lead anything he wants to lead, but South is going to draw trumps and claim the rest of the tricks.

Ask the Experts

You hold:

- ♠ K Q J 10 2
- ♥ K Q 10 8
- ♦ 6 5
- ♣ 7 3

A Connecticut reader asks what we think of an opening bid of one spade with this 11 high-card-point hand.

We slightly favor opening it, but have no criticism of anyone who prefers to pass with it. The hand is border line.

Overcoming entry problem

```
                NORTH
            ♠ 4 2
            ♥ Q J 7 6
            ♦ K 9 2
            ♣ 10 7 5 2
WEST                    EAST
♠ 10 3                  ♠ 9 6
♥ 9 5 4 2               ♥ K 10 8
♦ 8 5 3                 ♦ A J 7 4
♣ A K Q 3              ♣ J 9 8 6
            SOUTH
            ♠ A K Q J 8 7 5
            ♥ A 3
            ♦ Q 10 6
            ♣ 4
```

Vulnerable: Both
Dealer: South

West	North	East	South
			1 ♠
Pass	1 NT	Pass	4 ♠
Pass	Pass	Pass	

Opening lead:♣ K

When this hand was played in a team match both South players ruffed the second club and studied the play. It was easy to see that if West held the jack of diamonds the contract would make easily.

If East held that jack it might be possible to get to lead a heart from dummy and finesse against the king. In that case, the contract would still make.

One declarer didn't see a way to force an entry to dummy if East held both ace and jack of diamonds. He decided to run off a lot of trumps and hope that the defense would not be able to handle discarding problems.

He did just this, but somehow or other East and West managed to hang on to the correct cards and he lost two diamonds and a heart in addition to the club that went away at trick one.

The other declarer found the way to force an entry to dummy. He did play a few trumps and when he attacked diamonds he led the 10, letting it ride to the jack.

East returned a club. South ruffed and led his six of diamonds to dummy's nine. East took his ace and led his last club. South ruffed.

Now South got to dummy with the king of diamonds and finessed successfully against East's king of hearts to bring home game and a lot of IMPs.

Safety Plays

A safety play is designed to insure your contract against bad breaks. The use of these plays may cost you overtricks if there are no bad breaks but they really pay off over the years.

The last four of these hands are about a character named "Pessimistic Pete." Pete always gets bad breaks but guards against them successfully by some very unusual precautions. Incidentally, the safety play in hand five is one that anyone but a pessimistic Pete would overlook.

One poor play downs game

```
              NORTH
              ♠ 6 5
              ♥ 6 5 4 3
              ♦ Q 3 2
              ♣ Q J 4 2
WEST                    EAST
♠ K J 9 3               ♠ A 8 4 2
♥ 8                     ♥ 10 9 7
♦ J 9 8 7               ♦ K 10 6
♣ 9 7 6 3               ♣ 10 8 5
              SOUTH
              ♠ Q 10 7
              ♥ A K Q J 2
              ♦ A 5 4
              ♣ A K
```

Vulnerable: Both
Dealer: South

West	North	East	South
			2 NT
Pass	3♣	Pass	3♥
Pass	4♥	Pass	Pass
Pass			

Opening lead: ♠3

"Too bad you went into Stayman," said South. "I would have wrapped up three notrump. Of course, I was unlucky not to make four hearts. It took a spade lead, a misplaced spade jack, a 3-1 trump break and a misplaced diamond king to cook my goose."

"It also took a misplaced lack of playing ability to cause your downfall," replied North.

North was a trifle severe, but South had played like an optimist at a time when pessimism was called for.

East took his ace of spades and returned the deuce to South's 10 and West's jack. Now West led the king of spades.

South ruffed in dummy and started after trumps. When trumps broke 3-1 he could never get to dummy to discard his low diamonds on the queen-jack of clubs.

If South merely discarded a diamond from dummy on the king of spades, he would have been home. He could get in, draw trumps with three leads, cash the ace-king of clubs, enter dummy by overtaking his deuce of trumps with dummy's three, discard his losing diamonds and win the rubber.

Ask the Experts

A New York reader asks if we ever underlead an ace against a slam.

The answer is that if we do we don't do so often.

Safety scores honors

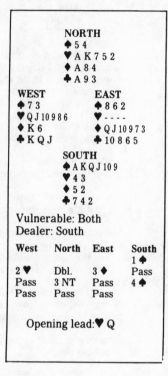

```
                NORTH
                ♠ 5 4
                ♥ A K 7 5 2
                ♦ A 8 4
                ♣ A 9 3
WEST                    EAST
♠ 7 3                   ♠ 8 6 2
♥ Q J 10 9 8 6          ♥ - - - -
♦ K 6                   ♦ Q J 10 9 7 3
♣ K Q J                 ♣ 10 8 6 5
                SOUTH
                ♠ A K Q J 10 9
                ♥ 4 3
                ♦ 5 2
                ♣ 7 4 2
```

Vulnerable: Both
Dealer: South

West	North	East	South
			1 ♠
2 ♥	Dbl.	3 ♦	Pass
Pass	3 NT	Pass	4 ♠
Pass	Pass	Pass	

Opening lead: ♥ Q

Californians take their bridge and politics quite seriously. So, when South looked at dummy and the opening lead he remarked: "I bid this hand like a supporter of Jerry Brown, but I am going to play it like a supporter of Ronald Reagan."

Suiting his actions to his words, he played the deuce of hearts from dummy. East who had been ready to ruff the ace or king simply discarded. The jack of hearts was led at trick two and another low heart was played. Along came the 10 — one more duck. Now South ruffed and drew trumps. Later on he scored dummy's ace-king of hearts and the other two aces to make the game he would have lost if he had tried to win the first trick.

"Well," said North. "I guess your opening spade bid represented Jerry Brown's liberalism, but you can't blame your four-spade bid on him. Your hand was going to take six tricks at either spades or notrump. I am not going to insult any current political figures by blaming them for that bid. Perhaps William Jennings Bryan might have approved it. All you did was to risk game and rubber in an effort to score 150 honors."

Safety play for contract

```
            NORTH
          ♠ A 9 5
          ♥ 7 5
          ♦ K J 9 5
          ♣ K J 4 2
WEST                EAST
♠ Q 10 2            ♠ J 8 7 6
♥ A Q 4 2           ♥ J 10 9 8 6
♦ 8 4 3 2           ♦ 6
♣ 10 8             ♣ Q 9 5
            SOUTH
          ♠ K 4 3
          ♥ K 3
          ♦ A Q 10 7
          ♣ A 7 6 3
```

Vulnerable: Neither
Dealer: South

West	North	East	South
			1 NT
Pass	3 NT	Pass	Pass
Pass			

Opening lead: ♣10

Here is an old hand that is well worth study.

You are in three notrump against a 10 of clubs lead. Can you play safe for your contract?

You certainly can, unless that lead happened to be a singleton. Just duck in both hands!

The actual hand shows East with three clubs to the queen. If he puts up his queen, South just plays his ace and gets four club tricks. If he holds the queen back, South gets only three clubs. But two spades and four diamonds get him to the magic total of nine.

If West has led from Q-10-9-8, South will play his ace of clubs next. East will show out and South will have a proven finesse.

And if West started with queen-10-small, the queen would drop on the third lead. South would collect one less trick than he could have scored, but his contract would have been safe.

Ask the Experts

You hold:

♠ J x
♥ x
♦ K J 10 9 8 x x
♣ Q 10 x

You respond two diamonds to partner's one-spade opening and rebid three diamonds after he goes to two notrump. He now bids three notrump. An Oregon reader asks what we would do.

We pass. We have told our partner that we don't like notrump. He has gone to three notrump in spite of that. Let him play it.

Unusual safety play pays

```
                NORTH
                ♠ A 5
                ♥ 7 3 2
                ♦ 7 5 3
                ♣ K Q 7 4 3
WEST                    EAST
♠ K Q 10 8 7            ♠ 9 6 4 3
♥ - - - -              ♥ Q 10 8
♦ Q 8 4 2              ♦ J 10 9
♣ J 9 8 6              ♣ A 10 5
                SOUTH
                ♠ J 2
                ♥ A K J 9 6 5 4
                ♦ A K 6
                ♣ 2
```

Vulnerable: Both
Dealer: South

West	North	East	South
			1 ♥
Pass	1 NT	Pass	4 ♥
Pass	Pass	Pass	

Opening lead:♠ K

The game was rubber bridge.

South went right up with dummy's ace of spades. He paused for study, led the deuce of trumps and finessed his jack after East followed with the eight.

West showed out. East glared and sputtered to South. "Stop peeking in our hands. If your ethics were as good as your eyes you would be one of the best men on earth."

"You have jumped to a wrong conclusion," said South mildly. "I saw no cards, but did see a perfect safety play to guarantee my contract once you followed to that first trump."

South had made an unusual safety play indeed. If he had played the ace or king of trumps he would have wound up losing one trick in each suit assuming proper defense by East and West. The unusual trump finesse avoided the trump loser.

Now suppose the finesse had lost to a singleton or doubleton queen. West would be on lead, but the seven of trumps would be a sure entry to dummy. South would have time to knock out the ace of clubs, get to dummy with that seven of trumps, discard his losing diamond on the good club and make 10 tricks instead of 11. But 10 tricks locked up the contract.

Hasty play sinks slam

```
                NORTH
                ♠ A K 5 3
                ♥ Q 6
                ♦ 7 6 4 2
                ♣ J 7 3
WEST                      EAST
♠ 7 4                     ♠ 10 9 8 6 2
♥ 8 2                     ♥ J 10 9 5
♦ K J 9 3                 ♦ 8 5
♣ 10 9 8 6 4              ♣ 5 2
                SOUTH
                ♠ Q J
                ♥ A K 7 4 3
                ♦ A Q 10
                ♣ A K Q
```

Vulnerable: Both
Dealer: South

West	North	East	South
			2♥
Pass	2♠	Pass	3 NT
Pass	6 NT	Pass	Pass
Pass			

Opening lead:♣10

"Haste makes waste" certainly is a good adage for declarer to follow when he is in a slam contract.

South wasted no time in hastening to lose his slam. As he explained slowly and carefully after the axe fell, it was really bad luck, but somehow or other the explanation fell on deaf ears as far as North was concerned. East and West accepted it gracefully.

South won the club lead, cashed his queen and jack of spades. He then entered dummy with the queen of hearts, discarded his queen-ten of diamonds on the ace-king of spades and started on the rest of the heart suit.

East held four hearts and the last spade and had to get those two tricks.

Do you see how South could have made the slam?

Fairly easy. At trick four he should have played low hearts from both the North and South hands. This would have cost him a 30 point overtrick against a 3-3 heart break, but given him 1440 points for making a slam against the five spade-four heart combination he was up against.

Sure thing approach wins

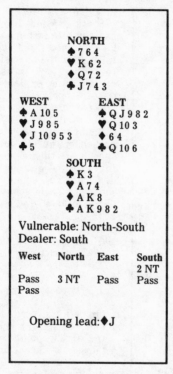

NORTH
♠ 7 6 4
♥ K 6 2
♦ Q 7 2
♣ J 7 4 3

WEST
♠ A 10 5
♥ J 9 8 5
♦ J 10 9 5 3
♣ 5

EAST
♠ Q J 9 8 2
♥ Q 10 3
♦ 6 4
♣ Q 10 6

SOUTH
♠ K 3
♥ A 7 4
♦ A K 8
♣ A K 9 8 2

Vulnerable: North-South
Dealer: South

West	North	East	South
			2 NT
Pass	3 NT	Pass	Pass
Pass			

Opening lead:♦ J

South's two notrump open-ing with 21 HCP was fully jus-tified by the texture of his hand with all points in aces and kings and a good five-card suit.

His first look at dummy showed 10 top tricks if he could run the whole club suit, and nine tricks if he could count on four clubs. He also saw that if East had three clubs to the queen and could get in with that card he might crush South with a spade lead.

South decided that he want-ed his contract and took a sure thing play to make it. He won the diamond in dummy, led the seven of clubs and let it ride after East played low.

When the seven held, South had his 10 top tricks. So he ran the clubs. East and West chucked diamonds so South cashed the ace-king. Then he played ace-king-small of hearts. By this time East and West had each thrown a heart, so West was in and had to give South a trick with the king of spades.

Note that South's play was sure to bring home nine tricks. If West held all four clubs, South would play high and lead back toward dummy's jack.

Of course, he would score one trick less than normal if West scored a club trick with the queen or 10, but safety wins games and sometimes, as today, overtricks.

A super safety play wins

```
              NORTH
            ♠ A J
            ♥ A K 6 3
            ♦ J 5 4
            ♣ 6 5 4 3
WEST                    EAST
♠ 10 8 6 5 3 2          ♠ K 7
♥ Q 9 8 7              ♥ J 10
♦ Q 8 6               ♦ K 9 7 3 2
♣ - - - -             ♣ Q 10 9 7
              SOUTH
            ♠ Q 9 4
            ♥ 5 4 2
            ♦ A 10
            ♣ A K J 8 2
```

Vulnerable: Both
Dealer: South

West	North	East	South
			1 ♣
Pass	1 ♥	Pass	1 NT
Pass	3 NT	Pass	Pass
Pass			

Opening lead: ♠ 3

Pessimistic Pete looked over the dummy happily. The hour was late. It was the last rubber of the evening and Pete expected to win it and go home.

"Can anything bad happen to me?" he asked himself. "Give East the king of spades and five diamonds to an honor. He can get in and lead a diamond from that five to an honor. Then, if I have to lose a club I can wind up two tricks down."

After this thought, Pete played the ace of spades from dummy. Now he could count at least four clubs unless West held all four of the missing ones plus two spades, two hearts and a diamond.

Then he saw that if East held all four clubs he could get in trouble unless he made the sort of safety play that he, Pete, was famous for.

At trick two he led a club from dummy and carefully covered East's seven with the eight. West showed out and Pete's pessimism was well-rewarded. He wound up making an overtrick on a hand that would have been set without the super-safety play.

Pessimistic caution pays

```
              NORTH
              ♠ J 7 5
              ♥ J 4
              ♦ K 9 5 2
              ♣ A K J 3
WEST                    EAST
♠ K Q 10 8              ♠ - - - -
♥ 6 3 2                 ♥ A 9 8 7 5
♦ Q 10 8                ♦ J 7 6 3
♣ 10 9 8                ♣ Q 7 6 2
              SOUTH
              ♠ A 9 6 4 3 2
              ♥ K Q 10
              ♦ A 4
              ♣ 5 4
```

Vulnerable: Both
Dealer: South

West	North	East	South
			1♠
Pass	2♣	Pass	2♠
Pass	4♠	Pass	Pass
Pass			

Opening lead: ♣ 10

Pessimistic Pete looked over the dummy with his usual pessimism. Looks easy," he thought. That is, unless someone has all four trumps. Everything bad can happen. I had better take out insurance."

Then Pete came to his hand with the ace of diamonds and led a low spade. West rose with the queen and when East showed out Pete was in a pessimist's heaven. The insurance had started to pay off.

Pete still had work to do. West led a second club. Pete played a heart to his queen after East ducked. A second low spade was won by West's king and a third club led. Pete ruffed, led a spade to dummy's jack and came to his hand by playing dummy's king of diamonds followed by a diamond ruff. Then it was easy to play his ace of trumps to drop West's 10, concede a trick to the ace of hearts and make his contract.

Note that Pete had to choose the right way to get to his hand to pick up that 10 of spades. Also note that if East had held all four trumps Pete would have been able to get out with just two trump losers by leading trumps from dummy.

Ask the Experts

You hold:

♠ A 4 3 2
♥ K Q 4
♦ Q J 6 5
♣ K Q

A Missouri reader asks what we bid after our right-hand opponent opens one spade. Everyone is vulnerable.

We pass. A bid is too likely to get us in deep trouble.

Pete ponders plight

```
                 NORTH
                 ♠ A Q 10
                 ♥ Q J 7 3 2
                 ♦ 8 5 3
                 ♣ Q 6
WEST                          EAST
♠ 9 7 2                       ♠ K J 8 3
♥ 8 4                         ♥ 9
♦ J 9 7 2                     ♦ Q 10 4
♣ K 8 4 3                     ♣ J 10 9 5 2
                 SOUTH
                 ♠ 6 5 4
                 ♥ A K 10 6 5
                 ♦ A K 6
                 ♣ A 7
```

Vulnerable: North-South
Dealer: South

West	North	East	South
			1♥
Pass	3♥	Pass	4♥
Pass	Pass	Pass	

Opening lead: ♦2

Pessimistic Pete looked over dummy. It was too bad that its distribution was an exact mirror of his own. He wished that somehow or other he could have reached three no-trump. No amount of bad luck could defeat that contract. Still, four hearts looked like a good contract. Could anything bad happen to him there?

Suppose East held both king and jack of spades. It's one chance in four but Pete always expected those one in four chances to be against him. Was there any way to guard against that? Pete found one.

He let East hold the first trick with his queen of diamonds. Now East returned the jack of clubs.

Pete wasted no thought on the chance that East had led from the king. He had a sure thing going for him and went up with his ace.

Two rounds of trumps came next. Then Pete cashed his ace and king of diamonds and led the seven of clubs.

West took his king and led a spade. Pete played dummy's 10. As expected, East took his jack, but had to give Pete the rest of the tricks.

Note that if Pete had played less pessimistically West would have been able to lead spades twice and defeat poor Pete.

Care & caution aid win

```
                NORTH
                ♠ 10 8 5 3
                ♥ A Q
                ♦ K J 7 3
                ♣ K Q J
WEST                     EAST
♠ K 2                    ♠ Q J 7 4
♥ 7 5 4 3 2             ♥ - - - -
♦ 9 6 5 2              ♦ A Q 10 8 4
♣ 5 3                    ♣ A 6 4 2
                SOUTH
                ♠ A 9 6
                ♥ K J 10 9 8 6
                ♦ - - - -
                ♣ 10 9 8 7
```

Vulnerable: Both
Dealer: East

West	North	East	South
		1♦	1♥
Pass	3 NT	Pass	4♥
Pass	Pass	Pass	

Opening lead: ♦2

Pessimistic Pete decided not to let his partner play in three no-trump. He felt that things were less likely to go wrong in a heart contract.

East covered dummy's jack of diamonds with the queen and Pete ruffed.

A quick study of dummy showed Pete that there could be nothing wrong with the lead of a trump to dummy's ace. Then East discarded a diamond and Pete stopped to think things over.

His first thought was that he should have thrown a low spade at trick one to guard against that five-zero trump break.

He said to himself, "I will be more careful in the future."

Then he saw that he was still sure of his contract.

He ran off the rest of the trumps and carefully discarded the king-queen-jack of clubs from dummy.

Now he led his 10 of clubs. East took his ace and led a spade, but Pete was now able to score three club tricks and the rubber.

Note that if Pete had not chucked all three of dummy's nice clubs there would have been no way to get more than two club tricks.

Squeezes and Other End Plays

The encyclopedia of bridge lists over fifty kinds of squeeze plays alone. There are probably many more that have not yet been catalogued.

The examples in this book show many of the simpler forms of squeezes and other end plays. They are tough, but not so tough that you can't learn to work them if you try.

Card reading at its best

NORTH
♠ - - - -
♥ A J 10 9 7 3
♦ K J 10 6
♣ Q 5 2

WEST
♠ J 10 6 3 2
♥ 8 6 2
♦ 5 4 3
♣ 7 3

EAST
♠ 8 7 5 4
♥ K Q
♦ 8 2
♣ 10 9 8 6 4

SOUTH
♠ A K Q 9
♥ 5 4
♦ A Q 9 7
♣ A K J

Vulnerable: Both
Dealer: South

West	North	East	South
			2 NT
Pass	3♥	Pass	3 NT
Pass	4♣	Pass	4♦
Pass	5♠	Pass	6 NT
Pass	Pass	Pass	

Opening lead: ♠ J

South's two-notrump opening bid was slightly off beat because he lacked a stopper in hearts, but it most clearly described in one bid his high-card strength and distribution. North showed both his suits, and his five-spade bid showed first- or second-round control in spades: in this case, a void. Although six diamonds was cold, six notrump was not a bad contract. It seemed to depend on West having either missing heart honor.

After the lead of the jack of spades, however, declarer was able to make the contract even though both heart honors were in the East hand.

After winning the opening lead, declarer led a heart to dummy's jack which lost to the queen. East returned a spade to declarer's second honor.

Declarer realized that the opening lead of the spade jack showed that West had the 10 of spades. Since that was the case, declarer cashed his four diamond tricks, his three club tricks and his third spade honor.

Now he was in a two-card end position. North had the ace-10 of hearts. East's holdings were unknown. South had the nine of spades and five of hearts. West had the 10 of spades and a heart.

At trick 12, South led his remaining heart to dummy's ace-10. West followed with the eight and declarer played the ace, dropping East's king and making the slam. Declarer had been lucky that East had started with just the king-queen in hearts, but he also had discovered that fact.

Since West was marked with the 10 of spades, declarer knew that a finesse for the heart king at trick 12 could not work.

Dynamite double squeeze

```
                NORTH
                ♠ J
                ♥ K 10 9 5
                ♦ 9 7 3 2
                ♣ A J 4 2
WEST                        EAST
♠ K 2                       ♠ 8 7 5
♥ Q 4 3                     ♥ J 6 2
♦ A Q J 10 6 4             ♦ 8
♣ 9 8                       ♣ K Q 10 6 5 3
                SOUTH
                ♠ A Q 10 9 6 4 3
                ♥ A 8 7
                ♦ K 5
                ♣ 7
```

Vulnerable: Both
Dealer: South

West	North	East	South
			1♠
2♦	Dbl.	Pass	3♠
Pass	4♠	Pass	Pass
Pass			

Opening lead: ♦ A

North's double of West's overcall was negative showing length in the unbid suits and eight or more points. Although South had only 13 points in high cards, he liked his good seven-card suit and jumped to three spades which North routinely raised to game.

West made a speculative opening lead of the ace of diamonds. He continued diamonds at trick two and East ruffed. Declarer won the king of clubs return with dummy's ace and took a trump finesse. West won with the king and played a club which South ruffed. It might now appear that declarer must lose a heart trick to go one off, but that is not the case.

The defense has no chance. As long as East has the queen of clubs, a virtual certainty, and West the high diamonds, declarer must prevail.

Declarer led four rounds of trumps coming down to the king-10 of hearts, the nine of diamonds and the jack of clubs in dummy. West had three hearts and a diamond queen remaining and East three hearts and the club queen. South now played his last trump. West had to discard a small heart to keep his queen of diamonds and declarer pitched the worthless nine of diamonds from dummy.

Then it was East's turn. He also had to let go of a heart to hold onto his queen of clubs. Declarer cashed the king, ace and the good eight of hearts for his 10th trick. He had made his game via a double squeeze.

It's Vienna coup time

```
                    NORTH
                ♠ A K Q 4 3
                ♥ Q 10 7 6
                ♦ 4 2
                ♣ A 3
WEST                            EAST
♠ 10 9                          ♠ J 7 6 5
♥ K 9                           ♥ J 8 5 3 2
♦ K J 10 9 7 6 5                ♦ 8 3
♣ 10 2                          ♣ 9 5
                    SOUTH
                ♠ 8 2
                ♥ A 4
                ♦ A Q
                ♣ K Q J 8 7 6 4
```

Vulnerable: Both
Dealer: West

West	North	East	South
3♦	3♠	Pass	4 NT
Pass	5♥	Pass	5 NT
Pass	7 NT	Pass	Pass
Pass			

Opening lead: ♦10

It was about a 100 years ago when an unknown described as the best player in Vienna made a slam by first setting up a card in an opponent's hand and then squeezing him. This type play has been called the Vienna coup ever since, although the Vienna squeeze would be a better name for it.

South's five notrump call guaranteed all the aces and North decided to gamble out seven notrump.

Based on the principle that when you start with 12 you should score 13, the grand slam is a good one. Based on the actual cards the play for the 13th trick is only fair because spades don't figure to break and the king of diamonds is surely misplaced for you.

South won the first spade in dummy and decided that East held four spades. Could he squeeze East on spades and hearts? Not likely since East was in back of dummy. How about playing West for both red kings and working a Vienna coup against him?

South ran off his seven clubs while chucking two hearts, two spades and a diamond from dummy. Then he cashed his ace of hearts to set up West's king. He cashed dummy's two high spades and made the last two tricks with his ace-queen of diamonds since West had to unguard his king.

Simple squeeze works

```
              NORTH
              ♠ Q 7 6 4
              ♥ Q 5 2
              ♦ A K J
              ♣ A 9 6
WEST                    EAST
♠ 8 5                   ♠ 9
♥ 9 7                   ♥ A K 8 6 4
♦ 10 7 6 4             ♦ Q 9 5 3
♣ 10 7 5 4 3          ♣ K 8 2
              SOUTH
              ♠ A K J 10 3 2
              ♥ J 10 3
              ♦ 8 2
              ♣ Q J
```

Vulnerable: Both
Dealer: East

West	North	East	South
		1♥	1♠
Pass	4♠	Pass	Pass
Pass			

Opening lead: ♥9

The Vienna coup is a simple squeeze against one opponent that is complicated by the fact that he is back of the hand that is doing most of the squeezing.

Like all bridge plays it goes back to the days of whist. In fact the play got its name because the best player in Vienna (name unknown) is supposed to have made it over 100 years ago.

North and South might well have found their way to three no-trump. We really can't find any serious fault with North's jump to four spades.

East took his ace and king of hearts and continued for his partner to ruff. Now West led a diamond.

South rose with dummy's ace, played three rounds of trumps and paused for study. He came to the conclusion that East held both the king of clubs and queen of diamonds for his vulnerable opening bid so a Vienna coup was needed.

He cashed dummy's ace of clubs to set up East's king and ran his last trumps while discarding the nine and six of clubs from dummy.

East had to chuck his king of clubs on the last trump in order to keep protection for the diamond queen and South's queen of clubs had become a winner.

A crisscross squeeze

NORTH
♠ J 3
♥ A K 8 2
♦ A 10 7
♣ A K 6 5

WEST
♠ A K Q 9 7 4 2
♥ J 9 3
♦ 5 3
♣ 10

EAST
♠ 8 5
♥ Q 10 7 6
♦ 6 2
♣ Q J 9 4 2

SOUTH
♠ 10 6
♥ 5 4
♦ K Q J 9 8 4
♣ 8 7 3

Vulnerable: North-South
Dealer: West

West	North	East	South
3♠	Dbl.	Pass	4♦
Pass	5♦	Pass	Pass
Pass			

Opening lead: ♠K

The beginner follows to two spades and wins the trump shift. Then he runs off 10 tricks or if he is in a hurry just shows his hand and concedes down one.

The man who knows a little about squeezes will also concede. He will see that East, in back of dummy, will be long in hearts and clubs and that a simple two-suit squeeze won't work.

The man who knows all about squeezes will expect to make his contract by means of a crisscross trump squeeze.

He simply runs off all but one of his trumps while discarding dummy's two small clubs. East will have to make three discards. Two will be easy. They will be the four and two of clubs. The third will be impossible. If he chucks another club, South will cash dummy's ace-kings of both suits. Then he will ruff back to his hand with his last trump and make the last trick with his last club. If East chucks a heart the ace-king of hearts and a heart ruff establish dummy's fourth heart.

Why didn't squeeze expert South claim right away? Because if West held three clubs the criss-cross squeeze could not be developed.

Lead sets up squeeze

```
                NORTH
                ♠ 10 6 4
                ♥ J 5 3
                ♦ A K J 10
                ♣ 9 7 2
WEST                        EAST
♠ K Q 7                     ♠ A 9 5 3
♥ Q 9 2                     ♥ 10 8 7 4
♦ 8 6 5                     ♦ 4 3 2
♣ J 8 4 3                   ♣ Q 10
                SOUTH
                ♠ J 8 2
                ♥ A K 6
                ♦ Q 9 7
                ♣ A K 6 5
```

Vulnerable: Both
Dealer: South

West	North	East	South
			1 NT
Pass	3 NT	Pass	Pass
Pass			

Opening lead: ♠K

The expert automatically looks for a squeeze on every hand when he has almost enough top cards. He knows, as everyone should, that the essence of a squeeze position is the need to produce just one extra winner.

In today's hand West leads his king of spades and the defense takes four spade tricks. West discards a diamond on the fourth spade and East leads a diamond since he realizes that lead can't hurt him.

Now let's look at the hand from South's viewpoint. He has exactly eight winners and at first glance only the drop of a doubleton queen of hearts can bring in his ninth trick.

Is there a squeeze? Yes, there may be. Suppose one opponent holds four clubs plus the queen of hearts. Not very likely, but definitely possible. Then a Vienna coup will bring the game home.

South, who has chucked a club from each hand on the fourth spade, wins the diamond and promptly cashes the ace and king of hearts and then runs the diamonds. On the last diamond West is squeezed.

Could the defense have beaten South by opening a club?

They probably would have, but they did start with the spades and set up the squeeze for declarer.

Extra chance overcomes odds

```
                NORTH
                ♠ 8 7 4 3
                ♥ J 8 6 2
                ♦ A K
                ♣ K 5 3
WEST                        EAST
♠ K 10 6                    ♠ A Q J 9 5
♥ K 10 9 7 4                ♥ Q 5 3
♦ 3                         ♦ 7 6 2
♣ 10 9 7 2                  ♣ Q 8
                SOUTH
                ♠ 2
                ♥ A
                ♦ Q J 10 9 8 5 4
                ♣ A J 6 4
```

Vulnerable: North-South
Dealer: South

West	North	East	South
			1♦
Pass	1♥	1♠	3♦
3♠	4♦	Pass	5♣
Pass	6♦	Pass	Pass
Pass			

Opening lead: ♠6

"Why did I bid so much?" thought South. "Not that the slam is sure to lose. A successful club finesse and a 3-3 club break is all I need. Or can I add an extra chance?"

Then South proceeded to add that extra chance. He ruffed the second spade, cashed his ace of hearts, led a trump to dummy, ruffed a heart, led a second trump to dummy, ruffed another

heart and then proceeded to run off all his trumps to come to a four-card ending. He held his four clubs, North his three clubs and the jack of hearts.

West might just as well have held his head on the table. He had to hang on to the king of hearts and therefore was forced to chuck a club.

Now South led a club to dummy's king and made the hand when East produced the queen on the second club lead.

South had developed the squeeze as an extra chance. He was lucky to find the queen of clubs with East, but the Gods of chance help those who help themselves.

Ask the Experts

You hold:

```
♠ A Q 7 6
♥ 7 3 2
♦ K J 9
♣ K J 4
```

A Mississippi reader wants to know what you should lead against a four-heart contract. Needless to say, your partner has never bid.

A trump lead is called for. Make your opponents attack your honor cards in the other three suits.

Card break read expertly

```
            NORTH
         ♠ A J 7 4
         ♥ A 9
         ♦ A K 7 5 2
         ♣ Q J
WEST                 EAST
♠ 8 2                ♠ Q 10 5
♥ 10 7 5 2           ♥ K 8 4 3
♦ Q 10 3             ♦ J 8
♣ A 9 6 5            ♣ 10 8 3 2
            SOUTH
         ♠ K 9 6 3
         ♥ Q J 6
         ♦ 9 6 4
         ♣ K 7 4
```

Vulnerable: Neither
Dealer: North

West	North	East	South
	1 ♦	Pass	1 ♠
Pass	4 ♠	Pass	Pass
Pass			

Opening lead: ♥ 2

Here is the sort of hand where almost anyone who gets to four spades is going to lose the trump finesse plus one trick in each side suit and be one trick short.

Nevertheless there is an alternate line of play that succeeds and a really astute declarer might just adopt it.

West opens the deuce of hearts. East's king wins that trick and back comes the deuce of clubs to West's ace. Another club is led at trick three and South is in dummy.

Now South decides that hearts and clubs are each going to break 4-4. He believes both those deuce leads. In that case if trumps and diamonds each break 3-2 the man with three trumps will hold just two diamonds.

Therefore, South decides to try an elimination play. He starts by cashing dummy's ace, king of diamonds and ace of trumps. Then comes a trump to his king. Some days the queen might drop but not this day.

Now South cashes his high heart and high club to discard two diamonds from dummy and leads a low trump. East is in with his queen and his last two cards are a heart and a club. He can lead either one, but South ruffs in one hand and discards the low diamond from the other to get away without losing a diamond.

Try to find the squeeze

```
              NORTH
              ♠ A Q 5 2
              ♥ A J 10 4
              ♦ A 10 2
              ♣ A 5
WEST                      EAST
♠ 7                       ♠ J 10 9 4
♥ 9                       ♥ 8 2
♦ K Q J 9 7 4 3           ♦ 6
♣ J 9 7 2                 ♣ K Q 10 8 6 3
              SOUTH
              ♠ K 8 6 3
              ♥ K Q 7 6 5 3
              ♦ 8 5
              ♣ 4
```

Vulnerable: Both
Dealer: West

West	North	East	South
3♦	Dbl.	Pass	4♥
Pass	6♥	Pass	Pass
Pass			

Opening lead: ♦K

Here is an unusual end play hand. South could develop a squeeze by ducking the first diamond except that East would proceed to ruff the diamond continuation to leave declarer in the soup before taking even one trick. Therefore, declarer must win the first diamond.

There are no finesses available and no way to rectify the count for a squeeze since West stops diamonds and East spades.

However, declarer can stumble into a ruff and discard situation that must win for him as long as East holds just one diamond.

He wins the first diamond and plays two or three rounds of trumps. Then he plays dummy's ace of clubs and ruffs dummy's other club. Now he goes after spades. When the suit fails to break he simply leads and loses the fourth spade.

East is on lead with nothing in his hand but clubs. He has to lead one. South ruffs in dummy and discards his diamond loser.

If you want to have some fun with the hand see if you can find the squeeze at six no-trump after West is allowed to hold the first diamond. You win the second diamond, play three rounds of spades and run hearts. Your last two cards will be the four of clubs and eight of spades. West will have to come down to one club to keep the high diamond. The 10 of diamonds is thrown from dummy and East must also come down to one club to keep the high spade. Dummy's two clubs are good.

Note that this squeeze will be broken up if West plays a club at trick two.

Accentuate the positive

```
              NORTH
              ♠ K 10 8 2
              ♥ A Q
              ♦ 7 3
              ♣ A J 9 6 2
WEST                      EAST
♠ Q                       ♠ 6
♥ 10 9 8 6                ♥ K J 5 3 2
♦ K J 9 8 6 2             ♦ Q 10 5 4
♣ 8 4                     ♣ Q 7 5
              SOUTH
              ♠ A J 9 7 5 4 3
              ♥ 7 4
              ♦ A
              ♣ K 10 3
```

Vulnerable: East-West
Dealer: North

West	North	East	South
	1♣	Pass	1♠
Pass	2♦	Pass	3♠
Pass	4♠	Pass	4 NT
Pass	5♥	Pass	5 NT
Pass	6♦	Pass	6♠
Pass	Pass	Pass	

Opening lead: ♥10

There are a lot of ways to bid today's hand. Seven is a reasonable contract. All South needs to do to make it is to finesse the winning way for the queen of clubs. Also,

if North holds the queen of clubs instead of the queen of hearts, there are no finesses needed.

Many players would have bid seven with the South hand after North showed two aces, but this South settled for six.

A finesser plays the queen of hearts at trick one. It loses to East's king. A red card comes back and sometime later South must go after clubs. A good guess as to which way to finesse and he is home with his slam. A bad guess and the slam has disappeared into that place from which no traveler returns.

A player who knows about end plays refuses to take the heart finesse. He rises with dummy's ace of hearts, leads a trump to his ace, cashes the ace of diamonds, leads a trump to dummy and ruffs the last diamond.

Now he leads a heart. It doesn't matter where the king is. Whoever wins the trick must either lead a club to take declarer's finesse for him or lead a red card for declarer to ruff in dummy and discard a club from his hand.

Ideal end play explained

```
                NORTH
                ♠ K Q J 3
                ♥ 8 6 4 3
                ♦ A 2
                ♣ Q 9 5
WEST                        EAST
♠ 7 4                       ♠ 6 5
♥ 9 5                       ♥ A K J 10 2
♦ Q 10 9 7 5               ♦ J 6 3
♣ 10 8 6 2                  ♣ K J 4
                SOUTH
                ♠ A 10 9 8 2
                ♥ Q 7
                ♦ K 8 4
                ♣ A 7 3
```

Vulnerable: East-West
Dealer: East

West	North	East	South
		1♥	1♠
Pass	3♠	Pass	4♠
Pass	Pass	Pass	

Opening lead: ♥9

South starts by losing two heart tricks. Then he ruffs the third with a high trump.

There is a simple play for the contract. All South has to do is to find the king of clubs in the West hand.

Unfortunately, a review of the bidding makes it almost a certainty that East holds that king. It is up to South to try to find a way to make East lead a club to him.

South plays two rounds of trumps and is delighted to find that trumps have broken two-two. Now he can work an end play against East.

He leads a diamond to dummy's ace. Back to his king and then a ruff of his last diamond. Now he leads the last heart from dummy. East wins and South discards a club.

If East leads the last heart, South discards his last low club and ruffs in dummy. If East leads a club, South lets it ride around to his queen. Either way, South makes his contract.

Ask the Experts

The bidding has gone: one heart-double-two hearts.
You hold:

```
        ♠ K Q 7
        ♥ 6 5
        ♦ A 8 4 2
        ♣ K J 9 7
```

An Alabama reader wants to know your correct bid.

This is easy. You should bid three hearts. Make your partner pick the suit. You can raise whichever one he bids.

East on the rocks

```
            NORTH
            ♠ A Q 9 8
            ♥ 8 6 5 3
            ♦ Q 8 6
            ♣ A 9
WEST                    EAST
♠ 7 5                  ♠ 4 2
♥ 9 7                  ♥ A K Q 10 2
♦ 10 9 5 4            ♦ K J 2
♣ Q 10 7 5 2          ♣ J 6 3
            SOUTH
            ♠ K J 10 6 3
            ♥ J 4
            ♦ A 7 3
            ♣ K 8 4
```

Vulnerable: Both
Dealer: East

West	North	East	South
		1♥	1♠
Pass	4♠	Pass	Pass
Pass			

Opening lead: ♥9

The defense started with three rounds of hearts. South ruffed the third lead high and drew trumps.

When they broke 2-2 South saw that if East held the king of diamonds he had a cinch end play against him.

Of course, the end play and the whole hand would collapse if West held that red king, but South had a lot of faith in the soundness of East's bidding.

As South explained after the hand was over, "If West held his nibs, I would have come out with egg all over my face."

South cashed dummy's ace of clubs, led a club to his king and ruffed his last club. Then came the end play.

He led dummy's last heart. East covered and now South discarded his three of diamonds.

Poor East was right between one of those rocks and hard places. If he led his last heart, South would chuck his seven of diamonds and ruff in dummy. If he led a diamond, South would let it ride around to dummy's queen.

Either way, East had given away a heart trick to get rid of two diamond losers.

Trump coup routs defense

```
                    NORTH
                    ♠ K 9 6
                    ♥ K Q J 7 6
                    ♦ Q J 9
                    ♣ 8 4
WEST                        EAST
♠ 5                         ♠ A J 4 2
♥ 8 5 3                     ♥ 10 9 4 2
♦ 8 7 4 2                   ♦ 6 3
♣ A K Q 6 5                 ♣ J 9 3
                    SOUTH
                    ♠ Q 10 8 7 3
                    ♥ A
                    ♦ A K 10 5
                    ♣ 10 7 2
```

Vulnerable: North-South
Dealer: South

West	North	East	South
			1 ♠
Pass	2 ♥	Pass	2 ♠
Pass	4 ♠	Pass	Pass
Pass			

Opening lead: ♣ K

The most advanced plays at bridge — like squeezes, end plays, trump coups — are thought to be in the realm of only the great players. However, bridge has developed so much since the 1920s that today all of these plays are familiar to most experienced players.

North-South easily climbed to their four-spade game contract. The defense started well. Three rounds of clubs forced declarer to ruff in dummy with the spade six. South's only problem was to guess the trump jack.

South led a heart to his ace at trick four and played a spade to the king, which lost to East's ace. East returned a diamond, which was won in dummy. Declarer led the spade nine and passed it when East followed small. West showed out!

South knew where the trump jack was but had no way of finessing for it as dummy no longer had any trumps. Declarer was no amateur. In an instant he found the winning line of play.

He led the king of hearts from the dummy and ruffed it small when East followed. Delarer was now down to the same trump length as East — two spades each.

South led a small diamond to dummy and when East followed small claimed the contract on a trump coup. South announced he would lead high hearts from dummy and discard his high diamonds on them until East ruffed.

South would then overruff and draw the last trump. East conceded and South had his game.

Misplays and Miscellaneous Plays

South loses game and temper

```
                NORTH
              ♠ 6 4 3
              ♥ 7 6 4 3
              ♦ Q J
              ♣ A 7 5 4
WEST                      EAST
♠ A Q J 9 8               ♠ 10 5
♥ 10 5                    ♥ J 2
♦ A 10 8 4                ♦ 9 7 6 5 3
♣ 9 3                     ♣ 10 8 6 2
                SOUTH
              ♠ K 7 2
              ♥ A K Q 9 8
              ♦ K 2
              ♣ K Q J
```

Vulnerable: Both
Dealer: South

West	North	East	South
			1♥
1♠	2♥	Pass	3 NT
Pass	4♥	Pass	Pass
Pass			

Opening lead: ♣9

South won the club lead in his own hand and looked at dummy for some time. Then he played three rounds of trumps. Two to pull them and the third just in case there might be an overlooked lurker somewhere.

Then he cashed his last two clubs and made the sneaky lead of the deuce of diamonds. If West had ducked South would have been in dummy to cash that ace of clubs for the tenth trick. Unfortunately for South, West clattered right up with his ace of diamonds and led a second diamond.

South was back in his hand and could do nothing better than to lead a low spade. East was careful to overtake his partner's eight with the 10 and to lead a second spade so South lost four tricks, game, rubber and his temper.

"Couldn't you let me play three no trump?" he asked his partner. "You had no singleton that I can see."

"Maybe I should have done just that," replied North. "Even an idiot like you would have made three no trump. But a bridge player would have made four hearts."

North was right. All South had to do was to lead his king of diamonds; not the deuce. If West played his ace he would have had to let dummy's queen be an entry. If West ducked, a second diamond would have end-played him.

Misplaying a sure thing

```
              NORTH
              ♠ A Q 9 7 3 2
              ♥ K 8 3
              ♦ - - - -
              ♣ 7 5 4 2
WEST                      EAST
♠ 8 4                     ♠ 5
♥ 9 2                     ♥ Q J 10 6 4
♦ Q J 10 9 6 3           ♦ K 7 5 4
♣ A K 9                   ♣ 10 6 3
              SOUTH
              ♠ K J 10 6
              ♥ A 7 5
              ♦ A 8 2
              ♣ Q J 8
```

Vulnerable: North-South
Dealer: South

West	North	East	South
			1♠
2♦	4♠	5♦	Pass
Pass	5♠	Pass	Pass
Pass			

Opening lead: ♦ Q

North remarked with considerable acerbity, "People who have no idea about how to play the dummy should not open with four-card major suits. Then maybe their partners could get to play the hand properly."

"I was just unlucky," replied South. "If East held either club honor, I would have made the contract."

South had drawn trumps and led a club from dummy. Later on he had led a second club to wind up with three club losers.

He was unlucky. He also had misplayed a sure thing contract.

At trick one he should ruff a diamond. Then a trump to his hand, a second diamond ruff, a second trump to his hand, a discard of a heart on his ace of diamonds, three rounds of hearts with the third one ruffed in dummy. Finally, after all that preparation, he then leads a club from dummy.

West would win that club, but would be stone cold dead. A red card lead would allow a ruff in one hand and a club discard from the other, and a club lead would set up a club trick for South.

Ask the Experts

You hold:

♠ 2
♥ A Q 8 7 6
♦ A K J 9 5 4
♣ 6

A reader wants to know if we prefer to open one heart or one diamond.

We open one diamond with this 6-5 distribution, but have no serious criticism of a one-heart opening.

Declarer does himself in

```
                NORTH
                ♠ 10 9 7
                ♥ Q 10 9 2
                ♦ 8 4 3
                ♣ 8 6 4
  WEST                    EAST
  ♠ 8 5 3                 ♠ - - - -
  ♥ A K J 8 3             ♥ 7 6 5 4
  ♦ Q 5 2                 ♦ K J 10 7
  ♣ Q 10                  ♣ K J 7 3 2
                SOUTH
                ♠ A K Q J 6 4 2
                ♥ - - - -
                ♦ A 9 6
                ♣ A 9 5
```

Vulnerable: East-West
Dealer: South

West	North	East	South
			2♠
Pass	2 NT	Pass	4♠
Pass	Pass	Pass	

Opening lead:♥K

The late George Kaufman once said that there were two ways to tell when a certain bad player held a good hand. First, his face would light up and then he would misplay it.

South's face lit up as he opened two spades. The first cloud appeared when partner responded two no trump and a real frown appeared when he saw the dummy.

He ruffed the heart lead and slowly and carefully ran off all his trumps. Unfortunately for South, East managed to hang on to three diamonds and three clubs and while South got 100 points for his honors he was still down one.

Do you see how South misplayed the hand?

Once that king of hearts was led South had been handed his contract on a silver platter.

He could set up a heart trick in dummy. He should ruff high, lead a spade to dummy's ten, note carefully that East had shown out, play either the queen, ten or nine of hearts from dummy and discard one of his minor suit losers. It wouldn't matter what West led then. South would lead a low spade, finesse dummy's seven if necessary, lead another heart from dummy, discard an appropriate loser and eventually get to discard one loser on what would become a good heart.

Pinpoint play nails game

```
                NORTH
                ♠ 9 4
                ♥ 9 7 6 4 2
                ♦ 10 6 2
                ♣ A 8 5
WEST                        EAST
♠ J 7 6 3                   ♠ Q 10
♥ A K J 10 3                ♥ Q 8 5
♦ 5                         ♦ J 8 3
♣ Q 10 6                    ♣ K J 7 3 2
                SOUTH
                ♠ A K 8 5 2
                ♥ - - - -
                ♦ A K Q 9 7 4
                ♣ 9 4
```

Vulnerable: North-South
Dealer: South

West	North	East	South
			1 ♦
1 ♥	Pass	2 ♥	3 ♠
Pass	4 ♦	Pass	5 ♦
Pass	Pass	Pass	

Opening lead: ♥ K

A couple of clairvoyants might get to four spades, which makes easily provided South ruffs the first heart, plays ace-king of spades and then plays diamonds. However, South found himself in the normal five-diamond contract.

He ruffed the heart lead and really gave a lot of thought to the right play. Of course, if spades were going to break 3-3 he could score an easy 12 tricks. But suppose they broke 4-2 and diamonds broke 3-1. What could he do to insure his game contract?

Finally, South worked out an unusual variation of the loser-on-loser play to bring home the bacon.

He led out three rounds of spades and carefully discarded a low club on the third one. West won and shifted to a club, but it was too late. South took dummy's ace, played one round of trumps, led a fourth spade and discarded dummy's last club. It didn't matter what the defense did; South was going to get to ruff his last club and the rest of his hand was now good.

Oh, yes! He could not make the contract against an original club lead.

Expert acrobatics

```
              NORTH
              ♠ 6 4 2
              ♥ 7
              ♦ 10 9 3 2
              ♣ K Q 10 9 5
WEST                    EAST
♠ J 10 9 8              ♠ Q 7 5
♥ J 5 4 3 2            ♥ A 10 9
♦ 7                     ♦ K 8 6 5
♣ 8 6 4                ♣ A 3 2
              SOUTH
              ♠ A K 3
              ♥ K Q 8 6
              ♦ A Q J 4
              ♣ J 7
```

Vulnerable: No one
Dealer: East

West	North	East	South
		1♦	Dbl.
Pass	2♣	Pass	2 NT
Pass	3 NT	Pass	Pass
Pass			

Opening lead: ♠J

Establishing dummy's long suit when there is no apparent entry requires bridge acrobatics. The auction needs some explanation. South's double followed by his two no-trump rebid promised 19 or 20 high-card points and a balanced hand with diamonds well stopped.

West chose to lead from his strong four-card spade sequence. South allowed West's jack of spades to win the first trick. He won the spade continuation with his king.

Now declarer led the queen of diamonds from his hand. If East wins his king, the hand becomes easy for South. Dummy's 10 of diamonds is an entry to the club suit. East did best by ducking both the queen of diamonds and the jack when declarer continued the suit.

South then led his jack of clubs to dummy's king and East had to withhold the ace. When the 10 of diamonds was led from dummy, East and South both played low. won with his king, cashed his two aces and exited with a club to East's ace. East, reduced to the ace-10 of hearts and a small club, had to give South a trick with the queen of hearts.

finish, East, reduced to the ace-10 of hearts and a small club, had to lead a heart and South scored the queen.

In all, South took two spades, two hearts, four diamonds and one club in his well-played game. East defended well and prevented declarer from using dummy's club suit. But South countered all of his fine defense by expert play.

Declarer hog-ties defense

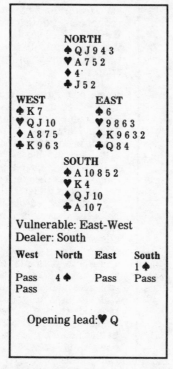

NORTH
♠ Q J 9 4 3
♥ A 7 5 2
♦ 4
♣ J 5 2

WEST
♠ K 7
♥ Q J 10
♦ A 8 7 5
♣ K 9 6 3

EAST
♠ 6
♥ 9 8 6 3
♦ K 9 6 3 2
♣ Q 8 4

SOUTH
♠ A 10 8 5 2
♥ K 4
♦ Q J 10
♣ A 10 7

Vulnerable: East-West
Dealer: South

West	North	East	South
			1 ♠
Pass	4 ♠	Pass	Pass
Pass			

Opening lead: ♥ Q

South wins the heart lead with dummy's ace and tries the spade finesse.

A second heart falls to his king and he draws the last trump.

He has lost one trick and must lose a diamond and one or two clubs. Can he do anything to keep his club losers to one? He sure can if East holds both king and queen or a doubleton honor. He also has various plays against West, but as you can see not one of these plays will succeed. Nevertheless there is a winning line of play.

Is it a squeeze or end play? No! It involves using the queen-jack-10 of diamonds to develop a trick.

South works on that suit and it doesn't matter where the ace and king are located.

South simply leads a diamond and lets either defender in.

The best defense will be another heart lead.

South ruffs, leads a second diamond, and discards one of dummy's clubs.

Now the defense has taken two diamond tricks instead of one, but South has established his last diamond as a winner. He can discard another club on it and will now be able to ruff both his small clubs in dummy.

Could East win the first diamond and lead a club to stop this? No. If the defense attacks clubs, South will only have one club loser.

Dummy reversal strategy

```
                 NORTH
                 ♠ K Q 3
                 ♥ Q 9 7
                 ♦ K 7 2
                 ♣ A 6 4 3
    WEST                      EAST
    ♠ 7 6                     ♠ J 10 9 5
    ♥ 6 5 3                   ♥ 4 2
    ♦ J 10 8 3                ♦ 9 4
    ♣ K Q 10 9                ♣ J 8 7 5 2
                 SOUTH
                 ♠ A 8 4 2
                 ♥ A K J 10 8
                 ♦ A Q 6 5
                 ♣ - - - -
```

Vulnerable: Both
Dealer: North

West	North	East	South
	1♣	Pass	2♥
Pass	3♥	Pass	3♠
Pass	4♠	Pass	5♦
Pass	6♦	Pass	7♥
Pass	Pass	Pass	

Opening lead:♣K

All roads lead to seven hearts with the North-South hands and the contract is a good one. You start with 12 top tricks and have 13 if either diamonds or spades break or if some sort of squeeze can be developed. Nothing breaks, no squeeze can be developed, yet seven is a cinch. There is a dummy reversal play available.

All you have to do is to trump three clubs in the South hand and then discard your fourth spade on dummy's third trump and your fourth diamond on the ace of clubs to come to 13.

You start by ruffing the first club. Now cash two trumps making sure to win the second one in dummy. Both opponents follow to the second trump so you don't have to worry about someone holding four of the little dears.

Ruff another club, enter dummy with a spade, ruff the last low club, enter dummy with a diamond and lead dummy's last trump to pull the last enemy trump and allow you, South, to get that spade discard. Now chuck a low diamond on the ace of clubs and claim the balance.

You have been able to score six trump tricks when only five appeared to be available.

A game with no guesswork

```
                NORTH
             ♠ A J 8 5
             ♥ Q 8 2
             ♦ A J 8
             ♣ 10 5 3
WEST                    EAST
♠ - - - -               ♠ 7 6 2
♥ J 6 4 3               ♥ A 10 9
♦ Q 7 5 3 2             ♦ 6 4
♣ J 9 8 2               ♣ A Q 7 6 4
                SOUTH
             ♠ K Q 10 9 4 3
             ♥ K 7 5
             ♦ K 10 9
             ♣ K
```

Vulnerable: Neither
Dealer: South

West	North	East	South
			1♠
Pass	3♠	Pass	4♠
Pass	Pass	Pass	

Opening lead: ♣2

The bidding was straightforward. Most people, superficially looking at the cards, would think the contract hinged on guessing the location of the queen of diamonds. This is not the case.

Declarer made the contract without guesswork. In fact, the defense was forced to do declarer's work for him.

East won the opening club lead with the ace, taking note that declarer dropped the king, quite obviously a singleton. Not wishing to help declarer in either of the red suits, and deciding against returning a club, East made the excellent switch to a trump.

South won the trump in dummy and made short work of the hand. He ruffed a club, played a trump to dummy's ace, ruffed dummy's last club and then drew East's remaining trump. With a trump remaining in his own hand and in dummy, South led a heart to dummy's queen.

East won with the ace of hearts and returned a heart. South smiled, knowing the hand was over. He won the trick with the king of hearts and exited with his remaining heart. The defense was now helpless.

It made no difference if East or West won the trick. The winner would be faced with a losing play. He would either have to give a ruff and sluff by leading a club or a heart, or he would have to lead a diamond solving the mystery of the diamond queen.

South never did learn who had the queen of diamonds. When he led his last heart he simply claimed the contract, showing the opponents his hand and explaining that there was no defense.

Uppercut artfully dodged

```
              NORTH
              ♠ Q 10 8 2
              ♥ Q 5
              ♦ A 10 8 6
              ♣ A 6 3
WEST                      EAST
♠ 4                      ♠ J 9 7
♥ A K J 10 6 4           ♥ 8 2
♦ Q 2                    ♦ J 9 7 4 3
♣ Q 9 8 5                ♣ J 7 2
              SOUTH
              ♠ A K 6 5 3
              ♥ 9 7 3
              ♦ K 5
              ♣ K 10 4
```

Vulnerable: East-West
Dealer: South

West	North	East	South
			1♠
2♥	3♠	Pass	4♠
Pass	Pass	Pass	

Opening lead:♥K

Here is another hand where you have to discard so as to avoid an overruff. Actually, it isn't necessarily an overruff, but a form of the play called an uppercut where if you ruff high you promote a trump trick for the defense.

South finds himself in a rather normal spade game after West has overcalled in hearts.

West leads the king of hearts and continues with the ace. East has played the eight first, so West continues with the jack.

You can ruff in dummy with the queen and pick up the spade suit if it breaks 2-2 or if the jack is singleton or you can ruff with the 10 and be in good shape if West holds the jack. Now, as a reader take a look at the East hand. He holds J 9 7 and either play loses.

Now let's get to the winning play. Why ruff at all? You see three clubs each in your hand and in dummy. If you ruff that heart you will still have to lose a club later on, so just chuck a club and let East and West whistle for another trick because they won't get one.

If another heart is led you can ruff in your hand. If anything else is led just win, play three rounds of trumps and eventually ruff your third club in dummy.

Defense cut down to size

```
                NORTH
                ♠ 6 5
                ♥ J 10 5
                ♦ J 10 8
                ♣ K Q J 10 9
WEST                      EAST
♠ 8 7 3                   ♠ 9
♥ Q 8 4 2                 ♥ 9 7 6
♦ K 6 4 3                 ♦ 9 5 2
♣ 5 4                     ♣ A 8 7 6 3 2
                SOUTH
                ♠ A K Q J 10 4 2
                ♥ A K 3
                ♦ A Q 7
                ♣ - - - -
```

Vulnerable: North-South
Dealer: South

West	North	East	South
			2♠
Pass	3♣	Pass	3♠
Pass	3 NT	Pass	6♠
Pass	Pass	Pass	

Opening lead:♣5

Here is one of those old-fashioned problem hands. South can make his slam against any lead, but a trump. He can't be beaten once a club is opened, but he has several lines of play that will probably succeed.

Let's look at the ordinary lines first. He ruffs the club lead, draws trumps and plays ace-queen of diamonds. East has followed to the first diamond with the deuce to show an odd number, so it isn't hard for West to duck. Now South leads a third diamond. West wins, gets out with his last diamond and waits for his queen of hearts to set the hand.

Suppose South starts by playing hearts. West must take his queen and lead a heart back. Still down one.

Now let's get to the line of play that wins against any defense.

South ruffs the ace of clubs high. Then he plays ace-king and deuce of trumps (note that East showed out on the king). Even if West has been smart enough to chuck the 8-7, he must win with the three.

Now he is stone cold dead. A club lead allows South to discard all his losers. A heart or diamond lead lets him in dummy to cash the clubs.

Note also, that this play should work against any combination of East and West cards.

Finding correct contract

```
                NORTH
                ♠ A K 10 9 7 3
                ♥ A J 9 2
                ♦ 6
                ♣ 5 3
    WEST                EAST
    ♠ J 8 4             ♠ Q 6 5
    ♥ K 8 3             ♥ Q 10 7 6 4
    ♦ Q 10 5 3          ♦ J
    ♣ J 10 9            ♣ K 7 6 4
                SOUTH
                ♠ 2
                ♥ 5
                ♦ A K 9 8 7 4 2
                ♣ A Q 8 2
```

Vulnerable: Neither
Dealer: South

West	North	East	South
			1♦
Pass	1♠	Pass	2♦
Pass	2♥	Pass	3♣
Pass	3♦	Pass	3 NT
Pass	Pass	Pass	

Opening lead:♣ J

Not all hands are compli-
cated. Frequently, getting to
the right contract is more difficult than playing it.

On the diagrammed deal,
three notrump could have
been defeated if West had
made an inspired heart opening lead. This lead would have
removed a vital entry to dummy and prevented declarer
from setting up the spade suit
and then enjoying it. Although
declarer would still have a
good chance of making the
contract, the 4-1 diamond
break would doom his chances.

After winning the opening
club lead, South maximized
his chances. He cashed the
ace-king of diamonds to deter-
mine how the suit was divided. If it had been 3-2, he would
give up a diamond and later
return to his hand with a club
to cash the remaining four
diamond tricks.

When diamonds failed to
divide, declarer turned to the
spade suit. He took the ace-
king of spades and played a
third spade. This time the suit
did divide.

In all, declarer took 10
tricks: 5 spades, 1 heart, 2 diamonds and 2 clubs.

This hand required timing.
Delcarer could not afford to
give up the lead more than
once. By taking the ace-king
of diamonds, he remained on
lead and was able to deter-
mine the best future course of
action.

Playing it by the book

```
                NORTH
                ♠ Q 7 5 3 2
                ♥ K 9 6
                ♦ A K 2
                ♣ 7 5
WEST                    EAST
♠ 6                     ♠ 9
♥ A J 8 7 4             ♥ 10 5 3
♦ J 10 9 7             ♦ 8 6 4 3
♣ K J 8                ♣ 10 9 6 3 2
                SOUTH
                ♠ A K J 10 8 4
                ♥ Q 2
                ♦ Q 5
                ♣ A Q 4
```

Vulnerable: North-South
Dealer: East

West	North	East	South
		Pass	1♠
2♥	3♠	Pass	4♣
Pass	4♦	Pass	5♦
Pass	6♠	Pass	Pass
Pass			

Opening lead:♦J

There is an easy way to play today's hand. Declarer plays a few rounds of trumps and takes the club finesse. West wins the king of clubs and cashes the ace of hearts and on to the next hand.

Can South do any better? There is a book play to gain one trick which will produce the slam.

It is a book play. In other words, it is similar to one that continually appears in bridge writings.

It is up to South to decide which opponent holds the ace of hearts. It would be a tough problem if it hadn't been for West's unfortunate decision to bid two hearts. It is the sort of bid that is really pointless. Once in a blue moon it helps West. Most of the time it doesn't affect the final result in any way, shape or form. This time it gives an alert declarer a sure thing play for the slam that might well have failed without West's overcall.

South knows where the ace of hearts is. He takes his queen of diamonds, draws trumps and leads his deuce of hearts.

Poor West is on the toasting fork. If he rises with his ace of hearts, South will get to discard one club on the king of hearts and the other on a high diamond. If West ducks, South will get to discard his queen of hearts on a high diamond.

Playing with blinders

```
                NORTH
              ♠ K Q 2
              ♥ A K 7 6 5
              ♦ K 4
              ♣ A 8 6
WEST                      EAST
♠ 8 3                     ♠ 9 6
♥ J 8 2                   ♥ Q 10 9 4
♦ Q 10 5 2                ♦ J
♣ J 10 9 5                ♣ K Q 7 4 3 2
                SOUTH
              ♠ A J 10 7 5 4
              ♥ 3
              ♦ A 9 8 7 6 3
              ♣ - - - -
```

Vulnerable: Neither
Dealer: North

West	North	East	South
	1♥	Pass	1♠
Pass	3♠	Pass	4♦
Pass	4 NT	Pass	5♥
Pass	7♠	Pass	Pass
Pass			

Opening lead: ♣ J

There is a special bridge astigmatism that causes the declarer to look so hard at part of a hand that he fails to consider all possibilities.

South studied the spade and diamond suits very carefully. He finally concluded that he should play two rounds of trumps before going after diamonds.

He discarded one diamond on dummy's ace of clubs, played dummy's queen of trumps, led a second trump to his 10 and relaxed when both opponents followed. Then he led a diamond to dummy's king and a second diamond to his ace. East showed out and South's grand slam had been sunk without a trace.

It had been an unnecessary loss. South had failed to see the extra chance that dummy's fifth heart gave him.

Once trumps broke, South should have played ace, king and then ruff a small heart from dummy. Back to dummy with the king of diamonds, another heart ruff and the grand slam would make. South's 13 tricks would be six trumps, ace-king of hearts, dummy's fifth heart, ace-king of diamonds, a diamond ruff and the ace of clubs.

Had hearts broken 5-2 South would still have been able to try for a 3-2 diamond break.

Ask the Experts

You hold:
♠ K J 8 4
♥ A K J 7
♦ 2
♣ K 9 4 3

A Carolina reader asks what opening bid we recommend.

This is easy. Open one club. This makes it easy for you to rebid.

Simple hand really isn't

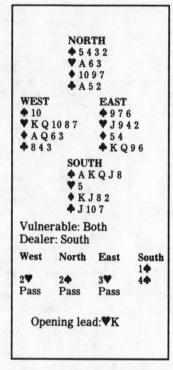

NORTH
♠ 5 4 3 2
♥ A 6 3
♦ 10 9 7
♣ A 5 2

WEST
♠ 10
♥ K Q 10 8 7
♦ A Q 6 3
♣ 8 4 3

EAST
♠ 9 7 6
♥ J 9 4 2
♦ 5 4
♣ K Q 9 6

SOUTH
♠ A K Q J 8
♥ 5
♦ K J 8 2
♣ J 10 7

Vulnerable: Both
Dealer: South

West	North	East	South
			1♠
2♥	2♠	3♥	4♠
Pass	Pass	Pass	

Opening lead: ♥K

Dr. T.B. Lyons, president of the American Bridge Teacher's Association, presents this hand in its quarterly. It is a simple enough hand, but we doubt if most players would find the winning line of play at the table.

Just look at the North-South hands and the bidding first. You win the heart lead in dummy, and your first thought is to play the 10 of diamonds and let it ride. This way you have a good chance to make an overtrick and a match-point player might well try it. But you are not playing match points and just want to make your contract.

Now look at all the cards and see the winning line to be sure of 10 tricks except against a 4-0 trump break.

Draw trumps and lead a diamond toward dummy. West will probably duck and dummy holds the trick. Lead a second diamond. West wins.

If he forces you with a heart, just lead a third diamond. He will take that trick, but now you will be able to discard one of dummy's clubs on your last diamond and wind up with just one club loser since dummy will be able to ruff the third club lead.

Suppose West shifts to a club after taking his queen of diamonds? Just duck; East can't lead a club back successfully and you will still get your club discard from dummy.

What do you do if West leads a club at trick one?

Pay off! That lead will defeat you.

South doesn't give up

```
            NORTH
            ♠ J 7
            ♥ A 6 4 3
            ♦ 8 6 4
            ♣ A K 8 7
WEST                    EAST
♠ K 10                  ♠ Q 8 2
♥ K Q J 9 7 5           ♥ 10 2
♦ J 5 2                 ♦ Q 10 9 3
♣ 10 5                  ♣ Q J 6 3
            SOUTH
            ♠ A 9 6 5 4 3
            ♥ 8
            ♦ A K 7
            ♣ 9 4 2
```

Vulnerable: Neither
Dealer: North

West	North	East	South
	1♣	Pass	1♠
2♥	Pass	Pass	3♠
Pass	4♠	Pass	Pass
Pass			

Opening lead: ♥K

South didn't like what he saw in dummy. It looked as if there were two sure losers outside the trump suit and two highly probable losers in trumps.

Still, there was no point giving up. South knew that there was a book play that might let him get away with just one trump loser.

At trick two he ruffed a heart. Then he led a low trump toward dummy. West went up with his king and led another heart.

South ruffed that one, entered dummy with a club and led dummy's jack of spades. East was helpless. If he covered, South's ace would pick up West's 10. If he ducked, the jack would be allowed to ride and later on South would drop East's queen under his ace.

Suppose West had played the 10 of spades on the first trump lead. West would have had to use his queen on dummy's jack and the ace would then pick up West's king.

South was lucky to find West with the 10 and a high trump. That was only a seven percent chance, but any chance is better than no chance at all.

4 Defense

Almost everyone knows that in defending against notrump you should attack in a long suit in the hope of setting up winners. In defending against suit contracts, the same principle applies although not with equal force. Just bear in mind that if you do attack dummy's long suits you may well develop low card winners for declarer. When you attack short suits with your side's long ones, you can only develop your own low cards.

In general, try to avoid opening new suits. The late Hal Sims once said, "Every time you break a new suit from declarer's left you lose half a trick on the average."

Leading through declarer and up to dummy's weakness is far better. You probably tend to gain when you do that.

In signalling strength, signal with the highest card you can spare, but never signal with a card that may be an important winner if you hang on to it.

Remember what the bidding has been. As soon as you see the dummy, add your and dummy's high card points to what declarer has shown and try to figure how many HCP your partner can hold. Then see if you can figure out the exact cards those points may represent.

Try to count everyone's distribution if you can and make it a point to protect jacks, tens, or even nines when it appears that they are important.

Then, while this may seem far-fetched and is hard to understand, don't throw low cards from nothing when it seems that declarer may have to work on that suit later on.

As an example, dummy shows king-jack-ten in a side suit. You hold 4-3-2. Don't throw one or two of those cards away carelessly. If your partner happens to hold the queen, you may be showing declarer where it is. Let him guess—don't draw a diagram for him.

Of course there is the converse. If you are declarer and have to find a queen, beware the ingenuous discard of a deuce. Maybe that player holds her ladyship.

Alert signaling pays off

```
                 NORTH
                 ♠ K Q 4
                 ♥ Q 9 6 2
                 ♦ K J 4
                 ♣ 7 3 2
WEST                        EAST
♠ A J 8                     ♠ 9 7 6 5 3
♥ 7                         ♥ 8 5 4
♦ A 10 9 7 5 2              ♦ Q
♣ J 5 4                     ♣ Q 10 9 8
                 SOUTH
                 ♠ 10 2
                 ♥ A K J 10 3
                 ♦ 8 6 3
                 ♣ A K 6
```

Vulnerable: Neither
Dealer: South

West	North	East	South
			1 ♥
2 ♦	2 ♥	Pass	4 ♥
Pass	Pass	Pass	

Opening lead: ♦ A

Back in 1935 the late Hy Lavinthal of Trenton, N.J., invented the suit-preference signal.

This convention is designed to help your partner decide which of two suits to lead when he will have an obvious choice.

This convention is valuable, but it is also difficult to use.

In his 1960 book Pierre Jais has a chapter that is the best writing on this convention we have ever seen.

His first example discusses the case when one is leading a suit that he expects his partner to ruff. This time West knows that his partner will ruff the second diamond. He also knows that left to his own devices, partner will return a club up to dummy's three small, rather than a spade up to dummy's strength.

Therefore, after West's ace of diamonds holds the first trick, he continues with the 10. His partner recognizes this as a call for the lead of the higher suit and does lead a spade. West takes his ace, leads another diamond and winds up with a well-deserved plus 50.

Wolf in sheep's clothing

```
              NORTH
           ♠ 8
           ♥ K 8 5 2
           ♦ A Q 6
           ♣ K J 10 5 2
WEST                    EAST
♠ Q 10 9 5            ♠ 7 3 2
♥ A Q 3              ♥ 4
♦ J 10 9 8           ♦ 7 5 4 3 2
♣ 7 4               ♣ 9 8 6 3
              SOUTH
           ♠ A K J 6 4
           ♥ J 10 9 7 6
           ♦ K
           ♣ A Q
```

Vulnerable: East-West
Dealer: South

West	North	East	South
			1♠
Pass	2♣	Pass	2♥
Pass	4♥	Pass	5♣
Pass	5♦	Pass	6♥
Pass	Pass	Pass	

Opening lead: ♥A

Most bridge players would double six hearts with the West hand. A few would take the conservative action of passing and opening the jack of diamonds.

Against all these players South would make the contract with correct play, which is to lead the jack of hearts and let it ride after West ducks. This play wins 50 percent of the time. If you rose with the king, your chance is somewhat less than 50 percent.

When this hand was played in a match-point game, every declarer except one made six hearts, although only about half the North-South pairs got beyond game.

At one table, expert South was playing against an apparent lamb who really was a wolf in disguise.

The wolf in sheep's clothing led ace and three of trumps. Can you blame South for hopping up with dummy's king?

We can't! Even though West's play is far from unreasonable.

Ask the Experts

You hold:

```
♠ A Q 2
♥ K 5 4
♦ Q 6 4 3
♣ A J 4
```

A Maine reader wants to know what you bid in response to your partner's opening notrump (16-18 points).

We just raise him to four. We have 16 points, but our distribution is 4-3-3-3 and our spot cards are about as small as possible. We only want to be in a slam if he holds a maximum.

High-level defense signal

NORTH
♠ 8 6 4
♥ A Q 10
♦ K J 8 7 4 2
♣ A

WEST   **EAST**
♠ A Q 7 2   ♠ J 10 5
♥ J 5 4   ♥ K 9 8 3
♦ 6   ♦ 10 9 3
♣ J 9 7 6 3   ♣ K 10 4

SOUTH
♠ K 9 3
♥ 7 6 2
♦ A Q 5
♣ Q 8 5 2

Vulnerable: Neither
Dealer: South

West	North	East	South
			Pass
Pass	1♦	Pass	1♥
Pass	2♥	Pass	2 NT
Pass	3 NT	Pass	Pass
Pass			

Opening lead:♣6

Bridge players should be familiar with the defensive principle which states: "When a defender signals with an honor he denies the honor directly above."

South had no satisfactory response over North's opening one diamond bid. He tried to muddy the waters with a psychic one heart response. He was paving the way for an eventual no trump contract and wanted to avoid a heart lead.

West led a club and East signaled violently with the ten. Although it is of no consequence here, East's play of the ten denies holding the jack.

South, with eight sure tricks, had to take a finesse in the suit he didn't want led, hearts, for his ninth trick. So he crossed to his hand with a diamond to his ace and led a heart to the queen and king.

East cashed the king of clubs and West played the jack, denying the queen. When East saw the jack of clubs, he knew that continuing clubs could only help declarer scoop up a quick nine tricks. East cleverly shifted to the jack of spades. Now the defenders were able to rattle off four spades and defeat the contract two tricks.

The key play for the defense was the jack of clubs, denying the queen. Without that bit of help, East would have no way of knowing that a club continuation was not the best.

Good defense is an art

```
            NORTH
            ♠ A J 9 7
            ♥ J 4
            ♦ K Q J 10 8 2
            ♣ 3
WEST                    EAST
♠ 8 6 3                 ♠ K 5
♥ K 8 7 3               ♥ 9 6 5 2
♦ 3                     ♦ A 9 6 4
♣ K J 8 4 2             ♣ 10 7 6
            SOUTH
            ♠ Q 10 4 2
            ♥ A Q 10
            ♦ 7 5
            ♣ A Q 9 5
```

Vulnerable: Both
Dealer: South

West	North	East	South
			1♣
Pass	1♦	Pass	1♠
Pass	4♠	Pass	Pass
Pass			

Opening lead: ♦3

Good defense looks so easy when it takes place that most declarers don't realize what has happened to them.

Take today's hand that was played in a rubber bridge game.

South gets to a very sound four-spade contract. It is so sound that there is a play for the spade slam. Just shift the East and West hands and the only defense against six would be for West to lead ace and another diamond.

At the table West did open his singleton diamond. East took his ace and his first thought was to give West the ruff he had asked for. Then he thought a little further and realized that the ruff would keep. It had to be important to set up another trick somewhere in case South held both missing aces. That somewhere had to be in hearts so at trick two East led a heart. Now there was no way to keep the defense from scoring the king of spades and the king of hearts plus the ace of diamonds (already taken) and that diamond ruff.

"Nice play, partner," said West.

"Deal," said South. "Everything happens to me, but some day a finesse will work."

Male chauvinist defeated

```
                NORTH
               ♠ 8 5 3
               ♥ 4 2
               ♦ A K Q 9 7 6
               ♣ 7 3
WEST                     EAST
♠ 10 9 6 2               ♠ 7 4
♥ 10 8 7                 ♥ Q J 9 6
♦ 8 2                    ♦ J 10 4 3
♣ Q J 10 8               ♣ 9 6 5
                SOUTH
               ♠ A K Q J
               ♥ A K 5 3
               ♦ 5
               ♣ A K 4 2
```

Vulnerable: Both
Dealer: South

West	North	East	South
			2 ♣
Pass	3 ♦	Pass	3 ♠
Pass	4 ♦	Pass	4 ♥
Pass	5 ♦	Pass	6 NT
Pass	Pass	Pass	

Opening lead:♣ Q

South's final bid of six notrump had little to commend it except that the game was match points and South wanted to get a top by playing notrump. In addition, South was a male chauvinist playing with a lady partner and men, whether chauvinists or not, tend to try to get the play away from partners of the other sex.

South won the club lead and quickly counted 11 top tricks. He would make all 13 if the diamond suit would run, but South decided to abandon all play for seven in an effort to give himself a chance for a squeeze to make six. So at trick two he led a low heart from his hand.

Unfortunely for South's dream of sugarplums, East was a very cagey player. He carefully overtook his partner's seven of hearts with his nine in order to lead the 10 of diamonds.

South's goose was cooked to a turn. He had to cash three diamonds right away and had no squeeze.

Now see what would have happened if East hadn't led that diamond. South would have cashed all spades and the last high club. East would have been forced to unguard diamonds or hearts and the slam would make.

Triumph with studious play

```
            NORTH
            ♠ 6 5 4 3
            ♥ K 7 3
            ♦ Q J 10 9 5
            ♣ 2
WEST                    EAST
♠ J 9 8 2               ♠ Q 10 7
♥ 9 6                   ♥ A 8 5 2
♦ 8 6 3                 ♦ A 7 4
♣ Q 10 6 4              ♣ 9 7 5
            SOUTH
            ♠ A K
            ♥ Q J 10 4
            ♦ K 2
            ♣ A K J 8 3
```

Vulnerable: Both
Dealer: South

West	North	East	South
			1♣
Pass	1♦	Pass	3 NT
Pass	Pass	Pass	

Opening lead: ♣2

If South had bid two hearts after his partner's diamond response they might just have reached the heart game which can be made against any defense. Still, we really can't fault South's jump to three no trump.

He won the first trick with the king of spades over East's queen and led the king of diamonds. West played the three and East ducked. He continued with the deuce of diamonds. West played the six and East took his ace, since West's order of diamonds play had shown three diamonds.

East led his 10 of spades and South took his ace. He led the queen of hearts. East ducked and the four of hearts was next led to dummy's king. East took his ace this time and was now at the key spot of the hand.

A careless player would lead the seven of spades. West would take his two good spades and be endplayed. He would have to lead away from his queen of clubs and South would romp home with three clubs, two spades, three hearts and a diamond.

East saw this danger and studied a while to decide between a club or heart lead. It didn't make any difference. As long as East didn't lead that seven of spades, declarer was doomed to defeat.

Tricks pay no interest

```
              NORTH
              ♠ 5 4 3
              ♥ J 9 6 3
              ♦ 6 4 3
              ♣ A Q 5
WEST                      EAST
♠ J 8 7 2                 ♠ Q 10 9
♥ A 8 4                   ♥ Q 10 7 2
♦ 7 2                     ♦ K 9 5
♣ 9 8 7 3                 ♣ K 4 2
              SOUTH
              ♠ A K 6
              ♥ K 5
              ♦ A Q J 10 8
              ♣ J 10 6
```

Vulnerable: Both
Dealer: South

West	North	East	South
			1♦
Pass	1♥	Pass	3 NT
Pass	Pass	Pass	

Opening lead: ♣9

East won the first trick with his king of clubs. He saw no future in the club suit and led back the 10 of spades.

The play proceeded quickly from then on. South entered dummy with a club, took a diamond finesse, returned to dummy with the other top club, repeated the diamond finesse and wound up with five diamonds plus two tricks in each black suit.

There was some discussion about the possibility that South could have made an overtrick if the defense had slipped, but no one noticed that East could have beaten the hand if he had simply played a low club at trick one.

Interest rates are high today, but no interest is paid on tricks at bridge. If East had ducked that first club, South would have had just one entry to dummy to lead diamonds. East would surely have made his king of diamonds and South would have been able to take only eight tricks.

Of course, the play might have proceeded very slowly. Maybe South would have found a way to get a trick out of his heart king, but in all probability he would not have worked that out.

Common unblocking sense

```
                NORTH
                ♠ Q J 10 8
                ♥ A K 7
                ♦ J 9 5 2
                ♣ 10 3
WEST                    EAST
♠ 5 4                   ♠ 7 3
♥ J 9 6 3 2             ♥ Q 10 4
♦ K 4                   ♦ Q 10 8 3
♣ Q J 9 7               ♣ 6 5 4 2
                SOUTH
                ♠ A K 9 6 2
                ♥ 8 5
                ♦ A 7 6
                ♣ A K 8
```

Vulnerable: North-South
Dealer: North

West	North	East	South
	Pass	Pass	1 ♠
Pass	3 ♠	Pass	4 ♣
Pass	4 ♥	Pass	6 ♠
Pass	Pass	Pass	

Opening lead: ♣ Q

It didn't take South more than a second to notice that his play for six spades was a mighty poor one. Then he proceeded to play the hand rapidly in a totally carefree manner.

He won the club, cashed his ace of spades, led a spade to dummy and noted that trumps had broken nicely.

Next came a diamond to his ace. No high diamond fell, but South was on his way to make the slam. He simply cashed his ace of clubs and ruffed the eight. Then he cashed dummy's ace-king of hearts and ruffed the seven. Now he led a low diamond. West was in with the king and didn't have another diamond to lead. He could lead a club or a heart, but it made no difference. South ruffed in dummy, discarded his last diamond and racked up game, slam and rubber.

West would have beaten the slam if he had just gotten rid of his king of diamonds under South's ace. Should he have made that play? The answer is a decided "Yes."

If South held either the 10 or queen of diamonds there was no reason why he should lead the ace. Suppose the diamond ace was singleton? Then East would hold queen-10-eight and be able to cover any diamond led from dummy later.

On trusting your partner

```
                NORTH
            ♠ K 10 8 4 3 2
            ♥ 9 2
            ♦ Q 2
            ♣ 10 6 3
WEST                      EAST
♠ - - - -                ♠ 9 7
♥ A K J 10 7 5           ♥ Q 8 3
♦ 8 5                    ♦ 10 9 4 3
♣ K 9 7 5 2              ♣ A Q J 4
                SOUTH
            ♠ A Q J 6 5
            ♥ 6 4
            ♦ A K J 7 6
            ♣ 8
```

Vulnerable: Both
Dealer: South

West	North	East	South
			1♠
2♥	2♠	3♥	4♠
5♥	5♠	Pass	Pass
Pass			

Opening lead: K♥

West bid up to five hearts and then retired from the auction. He had two good reasons to stop at that point. The first reason was that he might well have pushed his opponents one too high. The second reason was that for all he knew, it might turn out that a further push would get them to a makeable slam.

West opened his king of hearts and continued with the ace after his partner played the eight spot. When that held he looked around for new worlds to conquer. He had to shift to a minor suit. Which one?

It appeared to be a guess. At least West did guess and guessed wrong. He led a diamond and South had no trouble romping home with the rest of the tricks.

We aren't going into the merits of West's diamond lead except to point out one thing. It would be hard to visualize a holding where a club play would cost the contract. We do criticize West for his lead at trick two, however.

He should have led a low heart. His partner had raised him, had played the eight and almost surely held the queen. Put East in and he would have had no problem at trick three.

Ask the Experts

A Florida reader wants to know the origin of the expression, "Rubber bridge."

It goes back to whist where you would play the best out of three games. In case each side won one, then the third game would be called the "rubber" game.

Brilliant defensive play

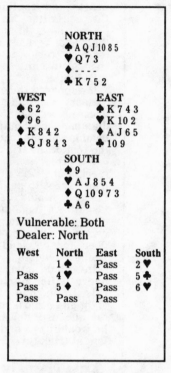

NORTH
♠ A Q J 10 8 5
♥ Q 7 3
♦ - - - -
♣ K 7 5 2

WEST
♠ 6 2
♥ 9 6
♦ K 8 4 2
♣ Q J 8 4 3

EAST
♠ K 7 4 3
♥ K 10 2
♦ A J 6 5
♣ 10 9

SOUTH
♠ 9
♥ A J 8 5 4
♦ Q 10 9 7 3
♣ A 6

Vulnerable: Both
Dealer: North

West	North	East	South
	1 ♠	Pass	2 ♥
Pass	4 ♥	Pass	5 ♣
Pass	5 ♦	Pass	6 ♥
Pass	Pass	Pass	

There is an Italian expression which translates roughly: "It may not be true, but it is well told."

This hand comes from Australia. The bidding is designed to get South to a rather poor heart slam.

Then we have West select a diamond lead, rather than a club.

South ruffs in dummy and leads the queen of trumps. East covers with the king and South lets it hold.

If East makes the rather normal play of a second trump, South draws trumps, leads a spade to the ace and continues with spades until East plays his king. After this, South winds up with a total of 12 tricks made up of five spades, one diamond ruff, two clubs and four trumps from his hand.

However, the Australian genius sitting East decides that South was dealt just one spade so he leads a spade right back. Declarer wins in dummy. His best play is to lead a spade. Genius East ducks. Now South can't ever bring in the spade suit since West holds the nine of trumps.

A really brilliant defensive play. One that just would not be made at the table because it would chuck the contract if South held two spades instead of just one.

Think, don't talk

```
                    NORTH
                    ♠ 10 5 3
                    ♥ A 7
                    ♦ A 8 4
                    ♣ J 10 9 8 6
    WEST                        EAST
    ♠ J 8 2                     ♠ 9 7 6 4
    ♥ Q J 10 9                  ♥ 6 5 2
    ♦ 6 3                       ♦ J 10 9 7 5
    ♣ K 7 4 2                   ♣ 5
                    SOUTH
                    ♠ A K Q
                    ♥ K 8 4 3
                    ♦ K Q 2
                    ♣ A Q 3
```

Vulnerable: North-South
Dealer: South

West	North	East	South
			2 NT
Pass	4 NT	Pass	6 NT
Pass	Pass	Pass	

Opening lead: ♥Q

South looked at dummy for a moment and commented, "Maybe we didn't bid enough." He could see 12 easy tricks with a 13th to come with some luck in the diamond suit.

Then, as frequently happens when a player uses his tongue instead of his brain, it turned out that he made only 11 tricks.

He won the heart lead with dummy's ace, led the jack of clubs and let it ride. West let it ride also. A second club came next and when East discarded South played his ace of clubs and continued with the queen.

Unfortunately for South, West was a thoughtful bridge player. He ducked again with his king. Some five minutes later, South had collected just 11 tricks and another slam had bit the dust.

South was a good sport. He congratulated West on his magnificent defense. North wasn't pleased at all.

He pointed out that while West had played well it had been most uncharitable of him to take advantage of a man who obviously belonged anywhere except at a bridge table.

As he explained, South should have played his queen of clubs on the first club lead and continued with the ace. Then he could lead the three. West could duck, win, whistle a happy tune or just give up. South would be able to win the third club in dummy, lead a fourth to knock out the king and have his 12th trick.

Discovering killing lead

```
              NORTH
              ♠ K 7
              ♥ 8 6 4 3 2
              ♦ A 9 8 2
              ♣ K 5
WEST                      EAST
♠ J 10 9                  ♠ Q 6 5 3
♥ A K                     ♥ Q J 10 9 7
♦ 7 6 4                   ♦ 5 3
♣ Q J 10 4 2              ♣ 9 3
              SOUTH
              ♠ A 8 4 2
              ♥ 5
              ♦ K Q J 10
              ♣ A 8 7 6
```

Vulnerable: Neither
Dealer: South

West	North	East	South
			1 ♦
Pass	1 ♥	Pass	1 ♠
Pass	1 NT	Pass	2 ♣
Pass	5 ♦	Pass	Pass
Pass			

Opening lead: ♥ A

Without an auction, if the West hand were given to 100 players on lead against a five-diamond contract all of them would lead a high heart. However, auctions are revealing. If West had drawn the proper inference from the diagrammed auction, he would have had an excellent idea of declarer's distribution. Then he could have found the killing lead.

South's bidding shows a three-suited hand of either 4-1-4-4 or 4-0-5-4 distribution. The modern tendency when holding three four-card suits as opening bidder is to bid the suit below the singleton in order to save room in the auction. North realized after South had bid three suits that his 10 high-card points were all golden and decided to jump to the diamond game, an action that was certainly justified.

West woodenly led his ace of hearts and the hand could no longer be defeated. He switchd to a trump at the second trick, but declarer was in control. South cashed his four black suit winners and scored six more diamond tricks by a cross-ruff.

If West had led a trump at trick one, which he should have realized was the right lead from the bidding, declarer would go down. South could still ruff two of his losers in dummy. But before he could ruff his third black suit loser, he would have to lead a heart as there was no quick entry to his hand. This would give the defense the chance to lead a devastating second round of trumps. South would be stranded with the two black suit losers as well as the heart loser.

The original heart lead effectively established communication between declarer and dummy for the cross-ruff.

The perfect opening lead

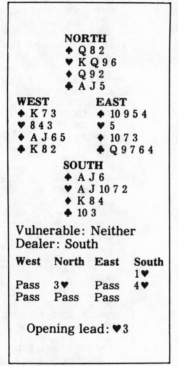

NORTH
♠ Q 8 2
♥ K Q 9 6
♦ Q 9 2
♣ A J 5

WEST   EAST
♠ K 7 3   ♠ 10 9 5 4
♥ 8 4 3   ♥ 5
♦ A J 6 5   ♦ 10 7 3
♣ K 8 2   ♣ Q 9 7 6 4

SOUTH
♠ A J 6
♥ A J 10 7 2
♦ K 8 4
♣ 10 3

Vulnerable: Neither
Dealer: South

West	North	East	South
			1♥
Pass	3♥	Pass	4♥
Pass	Pass	Pass	

Opening lead: ♥3

"There ought to be a law against an opening trump lead," complained South. "Any other lead and I would have been home free."

"We have too many laws now," replied West. "In any event a trump lead is clearly indicated with my holding."

It certainly was indicated and it certainly cooked South's goose. He had to lose a spade, two diamonds and a club. Now let's see what could happen with various other leads.

A club lead would be won by East's queen. Later on South would finesse successfully against West's king and get to discard a diamond.

A diamond lead would give South two diamond tricks instead of just one.

A spade lead would be won by South's jack. South would then draw trumps and play ace and six of spades. West would be back on lead with the king and forced to lead a diamond or club for South.

Ask the Experts

A Wisconsin reader asks if you can handle A J 3 2 opposite 10 7 5 4 so as to be sure of two tricks in the suit against any adverse holding.

Yes, there is a perfect and simple safety play. Just lay down your ace and continue with the deuce. If the suit breaks 3-2, all plays work. If there was a singleton honor it would have dropped. If either opponent held four to the king-queen he would score his king and queen, but that would be all.

Exception to the rule

NORTH
♠ K J 9 3
♥ A J 10 7
♦ 7 2
♣ J 7 4

WEST
♠ 7 5 4
♥ 8 5 2
♦ Q J 10
♣ A K Q 5

EAST
♠ 8
♥ K Q 9
♦ 9 8 6 5 3
♣ 10 9 3 2

SOUTH
♠ A Q 10 6 2
♥ 6 4 3
♦ A K 4
♣ 8 6

Vulnerable: Neither
Dealer: West

West	North	East	South
1♣	Pass	2♣	2♠
Pass	4♠	Pass	Pass
Pass			

Opening lead: ♣K

One of the first bridge lessons taught budding declarers is to draw your opponents trumps so that they won't be able to ruff your winners. Today's hand is an exception to this rule.

If the defense starts with three rounds of clubs South ruffs the third one. Then he can find a way to guard against finding both the king and queen of hearts with East.

He cashes one high trump and the ace and king of diamonds. Then he ruffs his last diamond and comes to his hand with a second trump, but must leave one with West. Then he takes and loses a heart finesse. But the defense can take no other trick. West can do nothing with his trump. East can't afford a heart lead. If he leads a club or diamond South ruffs in dummy and gets to discard one heart. Then he takes dummy's heart ace, ruffs a heart high, pulls the last trump and claims.

Could the defenders have beaten declarer? Yes, but it required exceptionally good play. East should follow to the first club with the nine and the second with the 10.

West would stop to think and realize that East was using a suit preference signal to ask for the higher side suit? It might look silly to lead a heart, but West would trust his partner and lead one. East would take the queen or king, lead a club or diamond and wait for his second heart trick.

An expert outsmarted

```
                NORTH
                ♠ A 7
                ♥ 10 9
                ♦ A K J 9 8 5
                ♣ A K 6
WEST                    EAST
♠ Q J 10 9 2            ♠ 8 6 3
♥ A J 8 3              ♥ Q 6 5 4
♦ 6                    ♦ Q 7 4
♣ 9 4 2                ♣ 10 8 5
                SOUTH
                ♠ K 5 4
                ♥ K 7 2
                ♦ 10 3 2
                ♣ Q J 7 3
```

Vulnerable: East-West
Dealer: North

West	North	East	South
	1♦	Pass	1 NT
Pass	3 NT	Pass	Pass
Pass			

Opening lead:♠Q

One of the first things a beginner learns is to return his partner's suit. Later on a student learns when not to return his partner's suit.

Then he is taught the general rule of leading fourth best, except from certain high-card combinations.

We now turn to our unlucky expert who sat South. We will let him tell his own story.

"On a good day I would have missed a slam, six diamonds plus my sure winners would have given me 12 tricks.

"The game was duplicate. Most other declarers at three notrump made 10 or 11 tricks at three notrump. I made just eight."

We will explain what happened to him. West made his normal lead of the queen of spades. Our unfortunate friend won in dummy and promptly played three rounds of diamonds.

This line of play was so standard that all other declarers did the same and all East players were on lead.

Those who always returned partner's suit led a spade and South made five odd. Those who realized that South was marked with the spade king led a heart. All but one led the standard fourth best. Declarer played low and made only four odd if West cashed a second heart.

Against our friend, East led the queen of hearts. A tough play, but the only one that could defeat the contract. South had no way to escape four quick heart losers.

Point counting aids East

```
              NORTH
              ♠ Q J 7 2
              ♥ K J 8 4
              ♦ A 9
              ♣ 10 6 4
WEST                    EAST
♠ 9                     ♠ K 8 6
♥ 10 7 6 3 2            ♥ 9 5
♦ 10 8 5 3             ♦ J 7 4 2
♣ K Q 2                 ♣ A 8 7 5
              SOUTH
              ♠ A 10 5 4 3
              ♥ A Q
              ♦ K Q 6
              ♣ J 9 3
```

Vulnerable: North-South
Dealer: South

West	North	East	South
			1 NT
Pass	2♣	Pass	2♠
Pass	4♠	Pass	Pass
Pass			

Opening lead: ♣K

The defense started off rapidly. West opened the king of clubs and continued with the queen and deuce. East was in with his ace.

Then came the pause that fails to refresh. East had a problem and even the simplest problem caused this East to take plenty of time.

East had something to think about. Normally it is really silly to give declarer a ruff and discard. Thus if East led the last club, declarer could ruff in his own hand and discard a loser from dummy.

Then East started to figure if there was any possible loser outside the trump suit. East started to count points. West had shown five. Dummy held 11 and East held eight for a total of 24 that declarer could not hold. North and South played normal 16-18 no trumps. East now counted jacks and found that he had seen all four. Hence, South could not have shaded his no trump to 15 points and surely would not shade it all the way to 14 when vulnerable.

Finally, East led his last club. South discarded a diamond and West ruffed with his nine.

Dummy had to overruff with an honor and now East was sure of a trump trick.

Bid and double gang

```
            NORTH
            ♠ J 9 5
            ♥ 6 3
            ♦ K Q 9 8
            ♣ Q 10 8 6
WEST                    EAST
♠ 8                     ♠ 6 4 3
♥ A K Q J 8             ♥ 10 9 2
♦ A 7 4 2              ♦ 6 3
♣ K J 5                ♣ 9 7 4 3 2
            SOUTH
            ♠ A K Q 10 7 2
            ♥ 7 5 4
            ♦ J 10 5
            ♣ A
```

Vulnerable: Neither
Dealer: South

West	North	East	South
			1♠
Dbl.	Redbl.	2♣	2♠
3♥	Pass	Pass	3♠
Pass	4♠	Pass	Pass
Dbl.	Pass	Pass	Pass

Opening lead: ♥K

West was a member of that group of bridge players who bid everything they can and then double their opponents.

Of course, this West had a mighty good hand for his bidding. Even with East's blank hand West would make eight or maybe nine tricks at hearts.

As for his final double, the less said the better, except that it was a bad percentage play. He wasn't going to set South more than one trick and there was no reason to expect to collect that small penalty.

Anyway, West did double and opened his king of hearts.

East followed with the deuce and West stopped to try to figure out any way to get four tricks out of what now appeared to be a collection of junk.

Finally, West saw a chance. At trick two he shifted to the deuce of diamonds. South won the trick in dummy and went into a slight trance.

He could see that West had found a way to beat his normally lay down contract. Then South cashed two trumps. He couldn't afford a third trump lead since that would leave him with his last two hearts as losers, so South led a second diamond.

West rose with his ace, gave his partner a diamond ruff and set the contract when East returned a heart.

Nine on the mind

```
              NORTH
              ♠ 10 2
              ♥ Q 10 9
              ♦ Q 3
              ♣ A 8 7 6 5 3
WEST                    EAST
♠ K 7 6 4               ♠ - - - -
♥ 8 6                   ♥ A J 7 5 4
♦ 10 9 6 5 4            ♦ A 7 2
♣ Q 10                  ♣ K J 9 4 2
              SOUTH
              ♠ A Q J 9 8 5 3
              ♥ K 3 2
              ♦ K J 8
              ♣ - - - -
```

Vulnerable: Neither
Dealer: South

West	North	East	South
			1♠
Pass	1 NT	Dbl.	4♠
Pass	Pass	Pass	

Opening lead: ♥8

South may have had nine-spot plays on his mind. In any event he played dummy's nine of hearts at trick one. East covered with the jack and South had to win with his king. He played the ace and three of trumps, but since East had shown out on the ace, West went right up with his king and led the six of hearts. East took his ace and gave his partner a ruff for the third defensive trick and the ace of diamonds was the fourth.

"Why didn't you play my queen of hearts at trick one?" asked North.

"I should have," replied South. "Just careless."

"You wouldn't have made the hand in any event," chortled East. "I had the killing play at my disposal."

Actually, it was a shame that East did not get a chance to put that killing play into operation. It would almost belong in a bridge hall of fame.

Had dummy's queen of hearts been played at trick one, East would have had to take his ace right then and there. Then he would lead back the jack of hearts. South would have been compelled to win with his king since dummy's queen had been played at trick one.

There would be no way to get to dummy to discard his third heart on the ace of clubs. When West got in with the king of trumps he would lead his diamond to East's ace and still get his heart ruff.

The South rises again

```
                    NORTH
                    ♠ Q J
                    ♥ A K J 10
                    ♦ A K Q 3
                    ♣ 6 4 2
WEST                            EAST
♠ A K 10 9 5 3                  ♠ 2
♥ 2                             ♥ 7 5 4
♦ 10 7 5                        ♦ J 8 6 4 2
♣ A Q 9                         ♣ 10 8 7 3
                    SOUTH
                    ♠ 8 7 6 4
                    ♥ Q 9 8 6 3
                    ♦ 9
                    ♣ K J 5
```

Vulnerable: Neither
Dealer: West

West	North	East	South
1♠	Dbl.	Pass	2♥
2♠	3♥	Pass	4♥
Pass	Pass	Pass	

Opening lead: ♠K

In the normal bridge game North and South will play some number of hearts. If they are good active bidders the contract will be four hearts by South.

West will start by leading out king, ace and 10 of spades. South will ruff with dummy's ace of trumps, cash the king and lead the jack to his queen. Then South will ruff his last spade with dummy's last trump and cash the three top diamonds to discard two of his three clubs. He will wind up losing two spades and a club and scoring his game.

There may be some comment about nice play, but no one is going to see that East could have defeated the contract.

Actually, East's play is simple once you notice it. He follows to the king of spades and then ruffs his partner's ace at trick two.

After that fine play it is no trouble for East to lead a club. West takes his ace and queen and South is one trick short.

North may suggest that South bid too much when he went to four hearts. Or if North is one of those rare souls who takes defeat with a smile he may congratulate East on his excellent defense.

Expert plays expertly

```
              NORTH
              ♠ 10 7 2
              ♥ 8 4
              ♦ K 9 3
              ♣ A K Q 10 2
WEST                    EAST
♠ 8 6 3                 ♠ A 5
♥ K Q J 6               ♥ A 10 7 3 2
♦ J 8 2                 ♦ 10 7 6 5 4
♣ 9 6 3                 ♣ 8
              SOUTH
              ♠ K Q J 9 4
              ♥ 9 5
              ♦ A Q
              ♣ J 7 5 4
```

Vulnerable: Both
Dealer: South

West	North	East	South
			1♠
Pass	2♣	Pass	3♣
Pass	3♠	Pass	4♠
Pass	Pass	Pass	

Opening lead: ♥K

"Another day, another dollar," remarked West.

"You're talking pre-war dollars," growned South. "You had nothing to do with setting me, other than to get off to your normal opening lead. It was East who put his hand in my pocket."

East had made a mighty good defensive play. It was one that any expert would feel rather proud of, not that an expert would think he had done anything sensational. It was merely that he had played well as experts are supposed to and usually do.

East carefully played his ace of hearts on his partner's king and returned his singleton club. South won in dummy and led the deuce of trumps. However, East hopped up with his ace and was now ready to return a heart. West was in with the jack and led a club for East to ruff for the setting trick.

It's nothing to ring bells about or to put East in the hall of fame, but the sort of fine defensive play that saves many a game for the players good enough to make it.

For those readers who think that four spades was a poor bid, we must point out that only super defense plus the 3-1 club break led to its defeat.

Defense con job succeeds

```
            NORTH
            ♠ A 8 4 3
            ♥ - - - -
            ♦ ,9 8 2
            ♣ A K Q 10 8 7
WEST                    EAST
♠ 9 7 6                 ♠ K Q J 5
♥ K J 8 5 3             ♥ A 10 9 7 2
♦ K 6                   ♦ 4 3
♣ 6 5 4                 ♣ 9 2
            SOUTH
            ♠ 10 2
            ♥ Q 6 4
            ♦ A Q J 10 7 5
            ♣ J 3
```

Vulnerable: Both
Dealer: North

West	North	East	South
	1♣	1♥	2♦
3♥	3♣	Pass	4♦
Pass	6♦	Pass	Pass
Pass			

Opening lead: ♥5

A very spirited auction in which all four players participated culminated in an excellent slam contract. Although North-South have only 23 high-card points, six diamonds is a good contract.

An original spade lead would almost surely defeat the slam because the diamond finesse is wrong, but West led a heart. However, he soon made up for his opening lead by making a terrific play. Even with all four hands exposed it is hard to imagine how West defeated the slam after his lead.

Declarer ruffed the heart in dummy and immediately took a diamond finesse by passing the nine. If West wins this trick, declarer will win any return, draw trumps and easily make the rest of the tricks. West knew that South had an excellent diamond suit because declarer had bid two diamonds followed by four diamonds. He realized his only hope of beating the slam would be a bold-faced swindle, but it had to be done quickly. Smoothly, West ducked the nine of diamonds.

Who could blame poor South for repeating the trump finesse? When West won his now unguarded king at trick three, the defense quickly cashed two heart tricks.

North: bitter and right

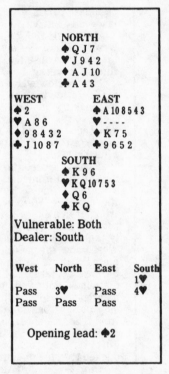

NORTH
♠ Q J 7
♥ J 9 4 2
♦ A J 10
♣ A 4 3

WEST
♠ 2
♥ A 8 6
♦ 9 8 4 3 2
♣ J 10 8 7

EAST
♠ A 10 8 5 4 3
♥ - - - -
♦ K 7 5
♣ 9 6 5 2

SOUTH
♠ K 9 6
♥ K Q 10 7 5 3
♦ Q 6
♣ K Q

Vulnerable: Both
Dealer: South

West	North	East	South
			1♥
Pass	3♥	Pass	4♥
Pass	Pass	Pass	

Opening lead: ♠2

North was bitter about the whole thing. He complained that he should have never raised his partner's heart opening bid with 4-3-3-3 distribution and stoppers in all suits.

North was right from a result standpoint. Playing in no-trump, he would have made four or five odd. Playing in hearts South fell short of his game contract.

We do sympathize with North but can assure him that year in and year out it is far better to raise hearts with his hand than to try to find a magic no-trump.

It took a lot of bad luck plus some fine defense for East and West to beat four hearts.

Actually, the fine defense wasn't difficult. West opened his deuce of spades. East took his ace and returned the 10. This was a suit preference signal to ask for a diamond return. So West ruffed and dutifully led back a diamond.

South's goose was cooked to a frazzle. He could do no better than take and lose the finesse. West got another spade ruff and his ace of trumps for down two.

Single suit play pays

```
              NORTH
              ♠ - - - -
              ♥ 8 6 5 4 3
              ♦ A K 9 4
              ♣ A 7 6 5
WEST                  EAST
♠ K 10 4 3            ♠ J 8
♥ Q 9 7              ♥ K J 10 2
♦ 10 3 2            ♦ Q J 8 7
♣ Q J 10            ♣ 9 8 2
              SOUTH
              ♠ A Q 9 7 6 5 2
              ♥ A
              ♦ 6 5
              ♣ K 4 3
```

Vulnerable: Both
Dealer: South

West	North	East	South
			1♠
Pass	2♥	Pass	2♠
Pass	3♦	Pass	4♠
Pass	Pass	Pass	

Opening lead: ♣Q

The really expert bridge player must learn all the correct single suit plays. This isn't too easy. In today's hand South made the correct series of trump plays and his knowledge paid off.

Four spades is not an out-standing contract, but it is going to make if trumps break 3-3. It will also make against certain 4-2 trump breaks.

South wins the club lead with his king and there is no reason not to play his ace of trumps at trick two.

He should note the fall of the eight before playing the next trump. Then it is up to him to get mileage out of his 9-7-6-5 by leading the queen next. It works this time because the queen picks up the jack and South gets off with the loss of just two trump tricks. If he leads the nine instead of queen he would lose to the jack, king and 10.

Wouldn't the queen play be a loser if East had been dealt K-8 instead of J-8? Yes, but the queen play wins against either the actual J-8 or the possible 10-8. Two chances instead of one.

Now suppose that the three and four had appeared on the ace. In this case the nine play picking up the king would be South's only chance. If the queen were led it could pick up the jack or 10, but the other defender would be left with the eight spot as a third winner.

5 The Professor

These seventeen hands are primarily educational and show the Professor teaching a bright student the finer points of the game.

Duck the opening lead

NORTH
♠ A J 6
♥ Q J 9 5 4
♦ J 4
♣ K 10 2

WEST
♠ 9 7 3
♥ 8 6
♦ Q 10 9 8
♣ J 8 7 4

EAST
♠ Q 10 8 4
♥ 7
♦ K 7 5 2
♣ A Q 9 5

SOUTH
♠ K 5 2
♥ A K 10 3 2
♦ A 6 3
♣ 6 3

Vulnerable: East-West
Dealer: South

West	North	East	South
			1 ♥
Pass	3 ♥	Pass	4 ♥
Pass	Pass	Pass	

Opening lead: ♦ 10

The student won the first trick with the ace of diamonds, drew trumps and led a club to dummy's king. East took his ace and queen and led a third club which the student ruffed. Later on, the student lost the spade finesse, a diamond and his game contract.

"I guess this isn't a good day for finesses," remarked the student.

"No it isn't," replied the Professor, "but once that ten of diamonds was led you were safe at home without the need for finesses."

All South had to do to insure his contract was to play dummy's jack of diamonds and let East hold the trick. East would play a second diamond. South would take his ace, ruff a diamond, draw trumps and lead a club to dummy's 10. East would be in with the queen and the second defensive trick, but there would be no way for him to get two more. A spade lead would cost the spade trick — a club lead would set up the king for a spade discard and a diamond lead would allow a ruff and discard.

We keep getting letters asking if you may pass your partner's Blackwood four notrump.

The answer is that the laws allow it but common sense dictates that you may lose a partner if you do.

94

End play scores contract

```
                NORTH
            ♠ 10 8 5 4 2
            ♥ K 7 4
            ♦ 7
            ♣ A J 7 4
WEST                      EAST
♠ K J 7                   ♠ 9 6 3
♥ A J 10 8 2              ♥ 9 6 5
♦ A 5 4 3                 ♦ 10 9 8 6 2
♣ 5                       ♣ 6 2
                SOUTH
            ♠ A Q
            ♥ Q 3
            ♦ K Q J
            ♣ K Q 10 9 8 3
```

Vulnerable: Both
Dealer: West

West	North	East	South
1♥	Pass	Pass	Dbl.
Pass	1♠	Pass	2♣
Pass	3♣	Pass	5♣
Pass	Pass	Pass	

Opening lead: ♦ A

West opened the ace of diamonds and continued the suit after East followed with the 10.

The Professor who was declarer said to his partner (the student), "You should have bid two hearts to suggest a notrump contract. Three notrump would have been a cinch, I have to work to make five clubs."

It wasn't really hard work for the Professor. He made the key play by discarding a spade from dummy at trick two so as to keep all three hearts there. Next came two rounds of trumps to take care of possible ruffs followed by the lead of the three of hearts toward dummy.

West was faced with a Hobson's choice. He could rise with the ace of hearts which would eventually allow South to take his queen of hearts and then discard the queen of spades on dummy's heart king; or he could duck.

He elected to duck. The Professor took dummy's king; came to his hand with a trump; discarded one of dummy's hearts on his last high diamond and led his queen of hearts.

West had to take his ace and was then forced either to lead a spade up to the ace-queen or a diamond or heart to allow a ruff in dummy and the discard of that spade queen from his own hand.

Ask the Experts

You hold:

♠ K x x x
♥ A x
♦ J x x x
♣ A x x

A Wisconsin reader wants to know the correct response to partner's one-diamond opening.

The correct response is one spade. You plan to bid again.

Student learns a lesson

```
              NORTH
              ♠ A K J 7
              ♥ A K 5 3
              ♦ 9 4
              ♣ Q 10 6
WEST                    EAST
♠ 8 3                   ♠ 6 5
♥ Q                     ♥ J 10 9 6
♦ K J 10 8 2            ♦ 7 6 5 3
♣ A K 9 4 3             ♣ 8 5 2
              SOUTH
              ♠ Q 10 9 4 2
              ♥ 8 7 4 2
              ♦ A Q
              ♣ J 7
```

Vulnerable: Both
Dealer: West

West	North	East	South
1♦	Dbl.	Pass	1♠
2♣	2♠	Pass	4♠
Pass	Pass	Pass	

Opening lead: ♣K

West opened the king of clubs and shifted to the queen of hearts after East had followed with the deuce.

The student won with dummy's king, drew trumps and led a second club to West's ace. West won and led a third club. South discarded a heart on dummy's queen of clubs and cashed dummy's ace of hearts and paused to regroup. Finally,

he led a diamond, finessed dummy's queen and was down one since he still had a heart to lose.

"What should I have done?" asked the student. "I knew that the diamond finesse was an almost sure loser, but beggars can't be choosers."

"You are right in one respect," said the Professor. "The diamond finesse was an almost sure loser, but your contract was perfectly safe if it did lose."

The student should simply have played his ace and queen of diamonds. West would take his king and be forced to lead a club or a diamond. The student would ruff in dummy and discard his last heart.

Ask the Experts

You hold:

♠ A Q 2
♥ K 8 7
♦ A Q 8
♣ J 7 5 3

A Michicagn reader asks our rebid after partner responds three hearts to our one-notrump opening.

We bid four hearts. Everyone likes to play notrump but we would look mighty silly if the opponents ran clubs against us.

Outsmarting the opponent

```
                NORTH
              ♠ K 10 7
              ♥ A 10
              ♦ K J 4 3 2
              ♣ 10 8 6
WEST                    EAST
♠ 9 6 5                 ♠ Q 4 3 2
♥ Q 9 7 5               ♥ J 6 2
♦ 9                     ♦ 10 5
♣ J 9 7 5 2             ♣ A K Q 4
                SOUTH
              ♠ A J 8
              ♥ K 8 4 3
              ♦ A Q 8 7 6
              ♣ 3
```

Vulnerable: Both
Dealer: East

West	North	East	South
		Pass	1♦
Pass	3♦	Pass	3♠
Pass	4♥	Pass	4 NT
Pass	5♦	Pass	6♦
Pass	Pass	Pass	

Opening lead: ♣5

The student won the club lead with the queen and continued with the king.

The Professor ruffed, drew trumps, played ace, king and another heart which he ruffed in dummy, ruffed dummy's last club and his last heart and was ready to look for the queen of spades.

He wasted little time in the process. He simply led dummy's king and then finessed against East.

"How did you figure that out?" asked the student. "I had already shown up with nine points in clubs and the jack of hearts. Didn't you think I would have opened the bidding if I also held the queen of spades?"

"I also knew that you are quite capable of false-carding," replied the Professor. "You could have won the first club with the king and played ace next to conceal the queen if you had wanted to hide that card. That could not fool your partner. So I knew you were going out of your way to show me your nine points in clubs. You wanted me to think that you could not possibly hold the spade queen so I played you for that card.

Ask the Experts

You hold:

```
♠ K J 5
♥ A K Q J 7 4 2
♦ 2
♣ 8 7
```

An Idaho reader asks if we would consider responding two hearts to our partner's one-club opening.

The answer is that we not only would consider a two-heart response, but we would **make** it.

Card lay dictates attack

```
                NORTH
                ♠ 9 7
                ♥ K 6 4
                ♦ K Q
                ♣ A K 9 6 5 4
WEST                        EAST
♠ 6 5 2                     ♠ 4 3
♥ Q J 10 8 5                ♥ 9 7 3 2
♦ 10 7 6 4                  ♦ A J 9
♣ 2                         ♣ Q J 10 8
                SOUTH
                ♠ A K Q J 10 8
                ♥ A
                ♦ 8 5 3 2
                ♣ 7 3
```

Vulnerable: Both
Dealer: South

West	North	East	South
			1 ♠
Pass	2 ♣	Pass	4 ♠
Pass	4 NT	Pass	5 ♥
Pass	6 ♠	Pass	Pass
Pass			

Opening lead: ♠ 2

The Professor looked at the deuce of trumps lead with evident distaste. Then he played dummy's seven and his own ace.

Next he cashed the ace of hearts at trick two and led a club to dummy at trick three.

Then came the key play of the hand. He discarded his last club on the king of hearts and ruffed a club with a high trump.

He entered dummy with the nine of trumps and ruffed another club.

Dummy's clubs were now good so the Professor cashed one more trump to pull West's last tooth and led a diamond to dummy's king-queen.

East took his ace, but the Professor still had one trump left to ruff a heart, whereupon dummy was good.

"You sure guarded against that 4-1 club break," said the student, "but wouldn't you have gone down if clubs had been 3-2 and trumps 4-1?"

"Not at all," replied the Professor. "When I ruffed the first low club I would have known that clubs were breaking 3-2. Then I would not have had to ruff a second club and could have handled a 4-1 trump break."

This is the sort of hand that is really instructive. Of course, the Professor had overbid his hand a trifle, but after you have played as well as the Professor has for as long as the Professor has you tend to overbid a trifle.

Canny defense dumps slam

```
                NORTH
                ♠ K
                ♥ J 9 5 4
                ♦ K Q J 6 4
                ♣ Q 6 3
WEST                      EAST
♠ Q 10 9 7                ♠ 8 6 4 3 2
♥ Q 10 6                  ♥ - - - -
♦ A 10 7 3                ♦ 9 8 5 2
♣ K 5                     ♣ 8 7 4 2
                SOUTH
                ♠ A J 5
                ♥ A K 8 7 3 2
                ♦ - - - -
                ♣ A J 10 9
```

Vulnerable: Both
Dealer: South

West	North	East	South
			1 ♥
Pass	4 ♥	Pass	6 ♥
Pass	Pass	Pass	

Opening lead:♠ 10

The Professor was a trifle surprised by the bidding, but did not even consider a double. He had too much strength. Also, he didn't know what to lead.

Most players would just open the ace of diamonds, but the Professor finally settled on the 10 of spades. South won in dummy and promptly led out the ace, king and a small trump. West was back on lead and faced with a really hard problem. Meanwhile East, who had played the deuce of spades at trick one, had made three spade discards.

Looking at all the cards you can see that a spade lead, a club lead or the ace of diamonds lead are all fatal.

The Professor worked this all out which finally led him to find the killing defense. He led a low diamond!

The Professor's computer mind had printed out the South hand as with three spades, six hearts, either no diamonds and four clubs or one diamond and three clubs. South would not have jumped to six if he would lose two quick diamond tricks.

Either way, the slam would not make. South might avoid a diamond loss, but he would still have to lose a club and if South was void of diamonds he could only get one discard on a diamond honor.

More on percentage play

```
                  NORTH
                  ♠ J 6 4 3
                  ♥ A 8 5
                  ♦ A 9 5 3
                  ♣ J 4
    WEST                      EAST
    ♠ Q 10                    ♠ A 5
    ♥ 10 6 4 2                ♥ K 9 3
    ♦ K J 10                  ♦ Q 8 7 6 4
    ♣ 10 8 3 2                ♣ K 6 5
                  SOUTH
                  ♠ K 9 8 7 2
                  ♥ Q J 7
                  ♦ 2
                  ♣ A Q 9 7
```

Vulnerable: Neither
Dealer: North

West	North	East	South
	Pass	Pass	1♠
Pass	3♠	Pass	4♠
Pass	Pass	Pass	

Opening lead: ♣2

The student put down his hand and said. "I guess I was a trifle weak for my limit raise, but I had passed as dealer."

The Professor said nothing. He never talked when declarer, but he planned to have a long discussion about limit raises later.

Then East produced the king of clubs and the Professor saw that as long as he could hold his trump losses to two he was going to make game. The hands fit perfectly and 22 high-card points were going to do the work of 26.

Therefore, he entered dummy with the ace of diamonds, led the six of trumps and let it ride to West's 10.

West shifted to the deuce of hearts. The Professor went right up with dummy's ace and led a second trump. The ace and queen fell together and the Professor happily conceded a trick to the king of hearts and claimed the balance.

The game was match point duplicate and the student asked, "Why didn't you rise with your king of trumps and make an overtrick?"

"I didn't need an overtrick," replied the Professor. "No one else will be in game and my play gave me a 94 percent shot at our contract."

Ask the Experts

A Wisconsin reader asks if we ever pass as dealer with 14 high-card points.

The answer is a decided "no". When we have the equivalent of one ace more than an average hand, there is too much chance that a pass will cost us a game.

An instructive hand

```
              NORTH
              ♠ 8 7 2
              ♥ Q J
              ♦ K Q J 7 4
              ♣ A J 10
WEST                     EAST
♠ 9 5 3                  ♠ 6
♥ 10 9 8                 ♥ 7 6 5 4 3 2
♦ A 10 9 2               ♦ 8
♣ K 9 3                  ♣ Q 8 7 5 4
              SOUTH
              ♠ A K Q J 10 4
              ♥ A K
              ♦ 6 5 3
              ♣ 6 2
```

Vulnerable: Both
Dealer: South

West	North	East	South
			1♠
Pass	2♦	Pass	4♠
Pass	5♣	Pass	5♥
Pass	6♠	Pass	Pass
Pass			

Opening lead: ♥ 8

The professor looked over the dummy with some distaste and broke his usual rule of silence by telling the student, "You should have let me play in four spades. Still, we will probably make our slam."

He won the heart lead and cashed two of his top trumps. Then he led a low diamond.

West ducked and dummy's jack held the trick. The Professor came back to his hand with dummy's last trump and led a second diamond. West ducked again, but the Professor was in charge. He returned to his hand with his other high heart in order to lead a third diamond. West had to win this one or lose his ace. Now dummy's last two diamonds were good and the slam came home.

This hand is quite instructive. The Professor's four-spade call was very descriptive. Solid trumps and eight winners without too much high card strength or slam interest.

The student should really have passed. He had extra values, but he should have discounted his queen and jack of hearts. When the student bid five clubs the Professor's five heart bid was correct. He was entitled to show heart control. Once started on his way to the stratosphere the student bid six spades.

A club lead would have led to quick defeat of the slam as would the lead of ace and a second diamond.

Finally, if the Professor had drawn three trumps he would have lost the contract.

Unusual play scores slam

NORTH
♠ A 6
♥ Q 10 7
♦ K 10 8 5 2
♣ 9 5 3

WEST   **EAST**
♠ K Q J 9 7 4 3   ♠ 10 8 5 2
♥ 8 6   ♥ A J 9 2
♦ 6   ♦ - - - -
♣ Q 10 4   ♣ K J 8 7 6

SOUTH
♠ - - - -
♥ K 5 4 3
♦ A Q J 9 7 4 3
♣ A 2

Vulnerable: North-South
Dealer: West

West	North	East	South
3♠	Pass	4♠	5♦
Pass	Pass	5♠	Pass
Pass	6♦	Pass	Pass
Pass			

Opening lead: ♠K

The student got up from his position as dummy to watch the Professor play the slam. He wondered what the Professor was thinking about. As far as the student could see there was only one line of play. Try to find West with the jack of hearts.

Let's join the student in seeing how the Professor made the slam in spite of the jack of hearts being wrong.

He discarded his low club on the ace of spades, ruffed a spade, cashed his ace of clubs, led a trump to dummy, ruffed a club, led another trump to dummy, ruffed dummy's last club, led a heart toward dummy and rose with the queen.

East took his ace and was caught in a total end play. A club or spade lead would allow South to ruff and discard a heart from dummy; a heart lead would run up to dummy's 10.

Why did the Professor adopt this unusual line of play? He was sure from the bidding that East held the ace of hearts. West's three-spade opening showed seven spades. He had played one diamond and three clubs so could not hold more than two hearts.

If one of them had been the jack, the simple play of leading toward dummy's 10 of hearts would have won and the Professor would have looked silly when his fancy play backfired, but experts play the percentages and the percentage play worked this time.

Bad contract well played

```
                NORTH
                ♠ 7 5
                ♥ Q 8 4
                ♦ 6 2
                ♣ Q J 10 8 3 2
WEST                        EAST
♠ 10 2                      ♠ Q J 9
♥ K J 9 7 6 2               ♥ A 10 5 3
♦ K J 9 4                   ♦ A Q 10 5
♣ 9                         ♣ 7 6
                SOUTH
                ♣ A K 8 6 4 3
                ♥ - - - -
                ♦ 8 7 3
                ♣ A K 5 4
```

Vulnerable: East-West
Dealer: East

West	North	East	South
		1♦	1♠
2♥	Pass	3♥	3♠
4♥	Pass	Pass	4♠
Pass	Pass	Dbl.	Pass
Pass	Pass		

Opening lead:♥7

The student ruffed the heart lead, thought for a longer period than usual and led a low trump. East won, cashed two diamonds and led a second trump whereupon the student drew trumps and claimed the rest of the tricks since dummy's long clubs would take care of his last diamond.

"A tough hand wasn't it?" asked the student. "I wasn't sure how to bid or play it."

"Your play was perfect," replied the Professor. "Your bidding was not. A club lead or diamond lead and a club return would have beaten four spades. Nothing could beat five clubs."

"Should I have doubled one diamond or bid four clubs over three hearts?" asked the student.

"No," was the reply. "But you should have doubled three hearts. This double is for takeout in modern expert practise and shows a strong hand with probably four cards in the unbid suit. One with which you could not double at your first turn because you couldn't stand for a heart bid by your partner. I would have bid four clubs in response to your double, you would raise me to five and against a heart lead I would have made all the tricks. A diamond lead would hold me to my contract, but no defense could defeat me."

Perfect timing plus luck

```
                NORTH
                ♠ 8 6 5 3
                ♥ A K 9 8 3
                ♦ A 5
                ♣ J 2
WEST                    EAST
♠ 10 4                  ♠ Q J 2
♥ 10 7 5 2              ♥ Q 6 4
♦ K 9 8 7 3            ♦ J 4 2
♣ 5 4                   ♣ Q 10 9 8
                SOUTH
                ♠ A K 9 7
                ♥ J
                ♦ Q 10 6
                ♣ A K 7 6 3
```

Vulnerable: Both
Dealer: South

West	North	East	South
			1 ♣
Pass	1 ♥	Pass	1 ♠
Pass	4 ♣	Pass	4 NT
Pass	5 ♥	Pass	5 NT
Pass	6 ♦	Pass	6 ♠
Pass	Pass	Pass	

Opening lead: ♠ 10

"How did you make the spade slam on board five?" asked the student.

"I just took the first twelve tricks," replied the Professor.

It wasn't quite as simple as that, but perfect timing plus a little bit of luck had let the Professer make his contract.

He started by cashing his ace and king of trumps. Then he went after clubs. The slam would be easy if clubs broke 3-3.

When West showed out on the third club, the Prof ruffed in dummy and went after hearts. Maybe someone held queen-10-small. That didn't work, but the Prof did get to ruff the third heart. Then he ruffed another club with dummy's last trump and led another heart. East could not afford to ruff so the Prof made his last trump and had 10 tricks in.

Now he led his last club and discarded dummy's five of diamonds to leave the ace of diamonds and a good heart in dummy. East could ruff and give dummy the last two tricks, but East simply chucked a diamond. Now dummy's ace of diamonds became the 12th trick and the Prof took it.

Restricted choice wins

```
                    NORTH
                  ♠ Q 8 4
                  ♥ Q 7 6 3
                  ♦ K 7 4 2
                  ♣ 7 4
WEST                        EAST
♠ J 10 9 2                  ♠ 7 5 3
♥ 10                        ♥ A J 8
♦ J 9 6 3                   ♦ 10 8 5
♣ A Q 10 5                  ♣ K J 8 2
                    SOUTH
                  ♠ A K 6
                  ♥ K 9 5 4 2
                  ♦ A Q
                  ♣ 9 6 3
```

Vulnerable: Both
Dealer: South

West	North	East	South
			1♥
Pass	2♥	Pass	4♥
Pass	Pass	Pass	

Opening lead: ♠J

Here is the Professor bidding his hand to the limit as usual. Many experts would merely have rebid three of some suit instead of jumping to game.

Had he rebid to three diamonds, North would have gone to four hearts. A three-heart rebid would undoubtedly find North passing.

The Prof won the opening lead in his own hand and promptly led a low trump toward dummy. West produced the 10 and dummy's queen fell to East's ace. The deuce of clubs came back. West took two clubs and led the 10 of spades.

The Prof won in dummy, led a trump and promptly finessed the nine after East played low. It held and the rest of the tricks were claimed.

"Horseshoes," murmured East.

"Just correct play," replied the Prof. "It was the use of restricted choice. West's play of the heart-10 was forced since he had a singleton. Had he held jack-10 he might well have played the jack. Thus my finesse was about a two-to-one favorite to win. Still I was lucky. Had I held the 10 of trumps instead of the nine, restricted choice would not have applied and I would probably have played for the 2-2 break and gone down."

Allergy leads to slam

```
                    NORTH
                    ♠ 6
                    ♥ A K J 3
                    ♦ A 5 3
                    ♣ A K Q 8 3
WEST                              EAST
♠ K Q J 9 8 5                     ♠ A 10 7 3
♥ 10 7 2                          ♥ Q 8 4
♦ 7 4 2                           ♦ 9
♣ 4                              ♣ J 9 7 5 2
                    SOUTH
                    ♠ 4 2
                    ♥ 9 6 5
                    ♦ K Q J 10 8 6
                    ♣ 10 6
```

Vulnerable: North-South
Dealer: West

West	North	East	South
2♠	Dbl.	4♠	5♦
Pass	6♦	Pass	Pass
Pass			

Opening lead: ♣4

The weak two bid is a popular modern invention to show a six-card suit and six-to-10 high-card points. West's two spades was right on the button for this bid.

North doubled for takeout and East jumped to four spades.

The Professor is allergic to being shut out. He bid a sporty five diamonds. West passed.

Then, North, looking at his rock crusher, went to six. He knew that the Prof liked to bid, but he also knew that the Prof played the dummy like Paderewski used to play the piano.

Had West opened the king of spades the Prof would win the second trick, ruff his last spade with dummy's ace of trumps, draw trumps and claim his slam. But West opened the four of clubs.

If it wasn't a singleton, South could draw trumps and clear the clubs for two spade discards. But the Prof was sure that it was a singleton.

He had to play three rounds of trumps to pull West's teeth and he just kept on with the rest of his trumps. His three discards from dummy were a spade, a heart and a club.

Meanwhile, East was having trouble. West chucked the king of spades to show that he held protection there. East chucked four spades and finally a club after one was thrown from dummy.

Now the Prof simply played out dummy's last three clubs. East took his jack, but had to lead away from his queen of hearts to give dummy the last three tricks.

Using the double finesse

```
                NORTH
              ♠ K Q 5
              ♥ 7 4
              ♦ K 6
              ♣ A Q 10 9 6 3
WEST                    EAST
♠ J 9 7 4               ♠ 10 3
♥ 10 8                  ♥ Q J 5 3 2
♦ J 8 5 4               ♦ A 7 3 2
♣ J 8 2                 ♣ K 7
                SOUTH
              ♠ A 8 6 2
              ♥ A K 9 6
              ♦ Q 10 9
              ♣ 5 4
```

Vulnerable: Both
Dealer: North

West	North	East	South
	1♣	Pass	1♥
Pass	2♣	Pass	2 NT
Pass	3 NT	Pass	Pass
Pass			

Opening lead: ♠ 4

The Professor let the spade come around to his ace. Then he led a club and double finessed with dummy's 10.

East took his king and led back a heart, whereupon the Professor rose with the ace, repeated the club finesse and eventually wound up with 11 tricks.

"Could we have held you to less?" asked the student who sat East. "Also, why did you play the ten and not the queen of clubs?"

"If you had ducked the first club, I could lay down dummy's ace and pick up the whole club suit. But I was not looking at all the cards. I would undoubtedly have come back to my hand with a high heart to repeat the double club finesse. You would take your king, knock out my other high heart and hold me to ten tricks since I would not have had time to knock out your ace of diamonds."

We are going to answer the student's second question.

The Professor played the 10 of clubs because it was the correct play. With split honors, he would have cost himself a trick if East held the singleton jack and gained one if East held the singleton king.

With both honors in one hand he would pick up the whole suit if West held king-jack-small, which was his extra percentage.

Dummy reversal nails slam

```
                NORTH
                ♠ 6 2
                ♥ K 9 8 4
                ♦ A Q 10
                ♣ K 8 4 2
WEST                        EAST
♠ J 9 7 3                   ♠ 10 4
♥ 5 3                       ♥ 7 6 2
♦ 9 8 7 5                   ♦ K J 4 3 2
♣ Q 10 6                    ♣ 7 5 3
                SOUTH
                ♠ A K Q 8 5
                ♥ A Q J 10
                ♦ 6
                ♣ A J 9
```

Vulnerable: Both
Dealer: North

West	North	East	South
	1♣	Pass	2♠
Pass	2 NT	Pass	3♥
Pass	4♥	Pass	4 NT
Pass	5♦	Pass	5 NT
Pass	6♥	Pass	Pass
Pass			

Opening lead: ♦ 9

The Professor looked over dummy and remarked, "There are so many ways to make this contract that I had best guard against as many bad breaks as possible. I'll be awfully embarrassed if I go down."

The student who was dummy got up, walked to where he could see the professor's hand, took a quick look at the West hand also and thought that with spades not breaking and all finesses wrong, the Prof might well be embarrassed.

The student gave a start when the Prof led the diamond ten from dummy at trick two and ruffed it with the ace of trumps. The queen and jack of trumps were played next with dummy's king overtaking the jack. Now the Prof ruffed dummy's queen of diamonds; entered dummy with the king of clubs; led dummy's nine of trumps to pick up the last adverse trump and went after spades. He ruffed out West's jack with dummy's last trump and made the last two tricks with the ace of clubs and his fifth spade.

The Professor had used a dummy reversal to be able to bring in six trump tricks instead of the mere five that were there if he had drawn trumps to start the proceedings.

Setting up needed tricks

```
                NORTH
              ♠ J 10
              ♥ A 10 6
              ♦ K Q 8 6 4 2
              ♣ Q 3
WEST                      EAST
♠ Q 9 6 4 2              ♠ 7 5 3
♥ 8 7 3                  ♥ 9 5 4 2
♦ 10 3                   ♦ A J 9
♣ K 10 9                 ♣ A 8 7
                SOUTH
              ♠ A K 8
              ♥ K Q J
              ♦ 7 5
              ♣ J 6 5 4 2
```

Vulnerable: Both
Dealer: South

West	North	East	South
			1 ♣
Pass	1 ♦	Pass	1 NT
Pass	3 NT	Pass	Pass
Pass			

Opening lead: ♠ 4

The student smiled happily when his jack of spades held the first trick. He had already left his seat on his way to watch the Professor operate.

He couldn't believe his eyes when the Professor played the deuce of diamonds from dummy at trick two.

East won with the nine and led a spade won by the Professor's king.

Now the Prof led a diamond toward dummy and rose with the king. East ducked but had to win the next diamond.

East led a third spade, whereupon the Prof wound up with three spades, three hearts, four diamonds, game, rubber and an overtrick.

"Why didn't you come to your hand with a heart at trick two and lead a diamond to dummy's king or queen?" asked the student.

"Because I wanted to win the rubber," was the reply.

This is the sort of hand that many players throw out the window. If a diamond is led to dummy's king, all East has to do is duck. Then he wins the second diamond and leads a spade. Diamonds are not set up. And since there is only one entry to dummy, that diamond suit is going to produce just that one trick taken at the start. South will wind up with seven tricks instead of nine or ten.

Early claimer justified

```
            NORTH
            ♠ A Q 6 3
            ♥ J 8
            ♦ Q 6 5 4 2
            ♣ K 9
WEST                    EAST
♠ 2                     ♠ 9
♥ Q 9 6 5 3             ♥ K 10 4 2
♦ 8                     ♦ K J 10 7
♣ Q 7 6 5 3 2           ♣ A J 10 4
            SOUTH
            ♠ K J 10 8 7 5 4
            ♥ A 7
            ♦ A 9 3
            ♣ 8
```

Vulnerable: Both
Dealer: East

West	North	East	South
		1♦	1♠
Pass	3♠	Pass	4♠
Pass	Pass	Pass	

Opening lead: ♦8

The Professor won the first trick with the ace of diamonds over East's 10. Trick two went to his jack of trumps. Both opponents followed and he spread his hand to claim his contract.

East looked it over carefully and said, "You mean you are down one, don't you?"

"Not at all," replied the Professor. "I have a cinch."

Then the Professor led his eight of clubs. Dummy's king lost to East's ace and a heart came back. The Prof took his ace, led a trump to dummy's ace, ruffed the nine of clubs and led his seven of hearts.

It didn't matter which opponent took that trick. If West won, he would have to lead a heart or club to give the Prof a chance to get rid of a losing diamond; if East won, he might cash his king of diamonds, but that would set up dummy's queen.

"Beautiful," exclaimed the student who was the North player. "But, wouldn't you have been set if West held a second diamond?"

"Of course," replied the Prof. "But if East held just three diamonds he would have had to have a five-card heart or club suit and would not have opened one diamond."

6 Hands About Actual People

Contract bridge won't be sixty years old until 1985. It is played by real people who just happen to sit North, South, East, or West. I have selected a few hands played by some of the great players.

While modern contract is a better and tougher game than that of the twenties and thirties, most of my actual people hands were played some years ago by old-timers. The youngsters will have the future after we are gone.

Finding the winning play

```
            NORTH
         ♠ K J 9 8
         ♥ Q 9
         ♦ 7 5
         ♣ K J 7 5 4
WEST              EAST
♠ 5 4 2           ♠ 3
♥ 8 3             ♥ 7 6 4 2
♦ K J 9 3         ♦ Q 8 6 4
♣ Q 10 8 2        ♣ A 9 6 3
            SOUTH
         ♠ A Q 10 7 6
         ♥ A K J 10 5
         ♦ A 10 2
         ♣ - - - -
```

Vulnerable: Both
Dealer: South

West	North	East	South
			2♠
Pass	3♠	Pass	4 NT
Pass	5♣	Pass	7♠
Pass	Pass	Pass	

Opening lead: ♠2

Jack Ehrlenbach, who became the first West Coast life master in 1946 when already 52 years old, died recently at the age of 85.

Jack was one of the most popular experts. Twice winner of the national mixed teams he won 23 West Coast regional events playing mostly with pupils. The keynote of Jack's game was simplicity. Of course, he mixed this simplicity with considerable masterminding. He had planned to bid only six spades if his partner had shown the ace of clubs.

Jack wasted no time in finding the wining play. He won the trump lead in dummy, ruffed a club, led the five of hearts to dummy's nine, ruffed a second club with the ace of trumps, led a trump to dummy, ruffed a third club with his last trump, led a heart to dummy's queen, cashed dummy's last two trumps in order to discard his 10 and deuce of diamonds and made the last four tricks with the ace of diamonds and good hearts.

Hands about actual people

```
              NORTH
           ♠ A K Q 10 9 8
           ♥ K Q 8
           ♦ J 3
           ♣ K 4
WEST                    EAST
♠ 6 4                  ♠ J 7 5 3
♥ 7 3 2                ♥ 6 5
♦ Q 10 6 4            ♦ 9 5 2
♣ J 10 9 3            ♣ Q 8 7 5
              SOUTH
           ♠ 2
           ♥ A J 10 9 4
           ♦ A K 8 7
           ♣ A 6 2
```

Vulnerable: North-South
Dealer: North

West	North	East	South
	1♠	Pass	2♥
Pass	3♠	Pass	4♦
Pass	4♥	Pass	5 NT
Pass	7♥	Pass	Pass
Pass			

Opening lead: ♣J

Helen Sobel was not only the best woman bridge player of all time, she was the equal of all but maybe two or three male players. Strangely enough, I always found myself playing against her until her last tourna-ment, the national mixed team of 1968. Helen was terminally ill at the time, but playing with my son Jim and Minda Brachman of Dallas we won going away. With all respect to Minda and Jim, Helen carried the three of us.

Our system was straight Helen. Strong no-trumps (points unspecified), limit raises (forcing raises to be worked out as needed) and just good card play. On our very first hand I sat South and had a problem at my third bid.

Way back in the early thirties, Ely and Jo Culbertson invented a convention known as the grand slam-force. It was too complicated for that day but it is in every expert bid kit today. Specifically my five notrump call asked Helen to bid seven with two of the three top honors in hearts. Needless to say we hadn't discussed anything this complicated but I knew that Helen would not pass. She thought for a second and bid seven hearts. Then, as she put down the dummy, she said "I hope you were looking for a trump marriage."

That was just what we needed and we had bid the only makable grand slam.

The lady from Atlanta

```
                NORTH
                ♠ A 2
                ♥ K J 10 6
                ♦ K 6 4
                ♣ A K Q 2
WEST                        EAST
♠ K 9 7 5 3                 ♠ J 10 6
♥ 9 3                       ♥ 7 2
♦ 10 9 8 7                  ♦ Q J 5 3
♣ 9 6                       ♣ J 10 8 4
                SOUTH
                ♠ Q 8 4
                ♥ A Q 8 5 4
                ♦ A 2
                ♣ 7 5 3
```

Vulnerable: Both
Dealer: West

West	North	East	South
Pass	1♣	Pass	1♥
Pass	2♦	Pass	3♥
Pass	4 NT	Pass	5♥
Pass	7♥	Pass	Pass
Pass			

Opening lead: ♦10

Except for Edith Kemp the only living woman to have won the Spingold is Margaret Wagar of Atlanta. Maggie won it in 1946 and 1948, but her string of women's and mixed victories started in 1940.

She has stopped serious play the last few years, but still appears occasionally to lend her charming presence to Atlanta tournaments.

Her 1948 win came with a pretty good team consisting of Sam Stayman, George Rapee, John Crawford and Howard Schenken.

We are not going to name whether Howard or John was the North player who put her in seven hearts in this hand from one of the early matches. Suffice to say, that if she had gone down the team would have been eliminated right then and there.

As you can see, there is no serious play for seven. Maggie studied dummy for a couple of seconds, but no one could tell from her expression that she was in trouble.

She took her ace of diamonds and led a trump to dummy's king. She returned to her ace and then led the queen of spades.

West ducked quickly and was conspicuously unsuccessful since Margaret let the queen ride and had stolen the grand slam.

We still sympathize with poor West, but must give our lady from Atlanta greatly deserved credit for devising and executing the lucky play.

Bridge's top women

```
                NORTH
                ♠ J 4
                ♥ A 5 3
                ♦ A K 10 8 6
                ♣ J 9 3
WEST                      EAST
♠ K 2                     ♠ 10 9 8 7 6 5 3
♥ K 10 8 7               ♥ 4 2
♦ 7 3                    ♦ 5 4 2
♣ K 8 7 5 4             ♣ 6
                SOUTH
                ♠ A Q
                ♥ Q J 9 6
                ♦ Q J 9
                ♣ A Q 10 2
```

Vulnerable: North-South
Dealer: North

West	North	East	South
	1♦	3♠	4 NT
Pass	5♥	Pass	5 NT
Pass	6♦	Pass	6 NT
Pass	Pass	Pass	

Opening lead: ♦7

The late Helen Sobel won both the Vanderbilt and Spingold cups. The only other woman to do the same is Edith Kemp of Miami.

Edith has been at the top for 40 years. Her style is aggressive. Hence, when East stuck in a non-vulnerable three-spade pre-empt Edith decided to overbid and got to six notrump on her own momentum.

West opened the seven of diamonds and Edith studied that lead. Why not lead partner's bid suit? Obviously, because you hold the guarded king. Why lead dummy's bid suit? Probably because you have the other two kings. What did that leave East for his three-spade bid? Favorable vulnerability and mild insanity.

So, Edith decided to play West for all three missing kings. At trick two she led her queen of hearts. West's king fell to dummy's ace. The nine of clubs was led and allowed to ride to West's king.

A second diamond was led. Edith won in her hand, cashed her ace of spades and last three clubs while discarding a heart from dummy. Then she ran dummy's diamonds. West had to throw two hearts in order to keep the king of spades. Edith had chucked her queen on one of the diamonds and the J-9 of hearts were the 11th and 12th tricks.

Mary was no dummy

```
              NORTH
              ♠ 10 7
              ♥ 9 8 6
              ♦ 10 7 5
              ♣ A Q 9 6 4
WEST                      EAST
♠ Q 9 5                   ♠ J 6 3 2
♥ K 10 3                  ♥ A Q J 7 5 4
♦ K J 9 8 3 2            ♦ Q
♣ 7                       ♣ 8 2
              SOUTH
              ♠ A K 8 4
              ♥ 2
              ♦ A 6 4
              ♣ K J 10 5 3
```

Vulnerable: Both
Dealer: South

West	North	East	South
			1♣
1♦	2♣	2♥	2♠
3♥	4♣	Pass	5♣
Pass	Pass	Pass	

Opening lead: ♥3

Mary (Mrs. Emory) Clement was one of the best woman players of the early 1930s. Mary preferred rubber bridge to duplicate. She died in 1936, so that her only real tournament success was to finish second in the 1935 national mixed teams.

Mary was a mild overbidder who compensated by really excellent dummy play. She worked squeezes, coups and end plays without ever admitting she knew what she was doing. Here is a hand from a rubber bridge game at Hal Sims' residence in Deal, N.J.

East won the first trick with the ace of hearts and led back the queen of diamonds. Mary took her ace. Her first thought was to concede down one and get on to the next hand. Then she saw a chance.

She drew trumps with two leads and ruffed a heart, cashed the ace and king of spades and ruffed a spade. Now she ruffed dummy's last heart with her next to last trump and led her last spade in order to discard one of dummy's two remaining diamonds. East, who had been dealt just one diamond, was forced to lead a heart. Mary ruffed with her last trump and discarded dummy's last diamond to make the last two tricks with dummy's trumps.

"Was that some sort of end play?" asked Mary while East fumed and spluttered.

Jo's grand slam force

```
                NORTH
                ♠ K Q 5
                ♥ K Q 10 9 7
                ♦ K 3
                ♣ 8 7 4
WEST                        EAST
♠ 9 3 2                     ♠ 8 6
♥ J 8 6 4 3                 ♥ 5
♦ J                         ♦ 10 9 8 7 6 5 4 2
♣ Q 10 6 2                  ♣ 9 5
                SOUTH
                ♠ A J 10 7 4
                ♥ A 2
                ♦ A Q
                ♣ A K J 3
```

Vulnerable: Both
Dealer: North

West	North	East	South
	1♥	Pass	2♠
Pass	3♠	Pass	5 NT
Pass	7♠	Pass	Pass
Pass			

Opening lead: ♦ J

No discussion of women bridge players would be complete without mentioning Josephine (Jo) Culbertson. She won the 1930 Vanderbilt, but had retired from active competition before the Spingold was first played.

Jo was the perfect partner for an active expert. Playing with Mike Gottlieb, Walde- mar von Zedtwitz or Louis Watson, she was always the very sound half of the partnership.

She was also the greatest exponent of the Culbertson system which she knew better than anyone.

In today's hand we show Jo using the grand slam force, which is still called the "Josephine" by some British writers because she actually invented it way, way back.

Her five-notrump call asked her partner, Louis Watson, to bid seven with two of the three top honors in spades and Louis did as she had asked.

Jo won the diamond lead with her ace, drew trumps and went after hearts. The 5-1 break meant she had only 12 top tricks, but Jo found the 13th on a squeeze. She cashed all her trumps discarding a heart and a club from dummy, led her queen of diamonds to dummy's king and discarded her three of clubs on the queen of hearts.

Jo had a perfect count on the hand since West had shown three spades, five hearts and a diamond. He was marked with four clubs, leaving just two for East. Since West had to retain the heart jack he had to come down to two clubs and the club queen was sure to fall.

Karn trophy winners

```
                NORTH
                ♠ A J 4
                ♥ 3
                ♦ K Q 9 2
                ♣ A 9 8 5 3
WEST                    EAST
♠ 6 5 3                 ♠ 10 9 8 2
♥ K J 10 6 4            ♥ Q 9
♦ 7 6 5 3               ♦ 4
♣ 4                     ♣ K Q J 10 6 2
                SOUTH
                ♠ K Q 7
                ♥ A 8 7 5 2
                ♦ A J 10 8
                ♣ 7
```

Vulnerable: North-South
Dealer: East

West	North	East	South
		3♣	Dbl.
Pass	4♣	Pass	4♥
Pass	4 NT	Pass	5♦
Pass	7♦	Pass	Pass
Pass			

Opening lead: ♣4

Back in 1931, the late Willard S. Karn gave a trophy for a Life Masters Individual Tournament limited to 36 players. The first seven winners were Karn (the trophy donor), Howard Schenken, David Burnstine, Elinor Murdoch, Oswald Jacoby, Waldemar von Zedtwitz and B.J. Becker.

The event was discontinued in 1960, but the winners read almost like a who's who of bridge, except that until Silvia Stein of Detroit won in 1958 no other woman managed to win. Elinor still lives in Birmingham where she occasionally plays in tournaments.

Here is one of the hands that helped her win the 1934 individual. The bidding was what might be expected from a 1934 individual and Elinor found herself in seven diamonds.

Dummy's ace of clubs won the first trick. Elinor saw that she needed to make all eight trumps separately in order to come to 13. She thanked the gods of chance for not having inspired West to lead a trump and proceeded to use perfect cross-ruff technique by cashing all her top spades and the club and heart aces.

Then she ruffed a heart with dummy's deuce of trumps and was able to claim the last seven tricks since her trumps were high and could be scored separately.

Bridge at 80-plus

```
              NORTH
            ♠ K 8 2
            ♥ Q J 9 6
            ♦ 7 4
            ♣ A K 10 3
WEST                    EAST
♠ Q 6 5 3              ♠ J 10 9 4
♥ 10 3 2              ♥ 7
♦ Q 8 6 2            ♦ A 10 9 5
♣ 7 4                ♣ J 9 6 5
              SOUTH
            ♠ A 7
            ♥ A K 8 5 4
            ♦ K J 3
            ♣ Q 8 2
```

Vulnerable: Both
Dealer: North

West	North	East	South
	1♣	Pass	1♥
Pass	2♥	Pass	2♠
Pass	4♥	Pass	5♦
Pass	5♥	Pass	6♥
Pass	Pass	Pass	

Opening lead: ♦2

For a couple of years Ted Lightner was unquestionably the best bridge player over 80 years old. Then Waldemar von Zedtwitz took his place.

Waldy, who is almost 86, still has a tremendous bridge knowledge and ability, but bad eyesight has made it impossible for him to play any more.

Today the best player over 80 is Albert "Dingy" Weiss of Miami. His national wins include two Vanderbilts and three pairs events, his seconds include two Spingolds. He confines his play to rubber bridge these days and is still a fine partner and a mighty tough opponent.

Here we see him in recent rubber bridge action. His two-spade call was to find out whether his partner could show any more than a minimum.

Why didn't he bid Blackwood? He was going to bid just six, even if his partner showed two aces.

Look at the opening lead. With the diamond lead, the slam was home free. Without a diamond lead, he would have had to make a good guess in the suit.

One thing in which Dingy has always excelled is getting his opponents to help him. He knew this West would assume the five-diamond call had been made to stop a diamond lead and therefore West would go out of his way to lead a diamond.

The Four Aces return

```
              NORTH
              ♠ K Q 7 6 5
              ♥ 8
              ♦ K 9 8 4 2
              ♣ 6 3
WEST                      EAST
♠ J 8 3 2                 ♠ 10 9 4
♥ J 9 7 4                 ♥ 10 6 5 3
♦ Q 10 6 3               ♦ J 7 5
♣ Q                       ♣ A 4 2
              SOUTH
              ♠ A
              ♥ A K Q 2
              ♦ A
              ♣ K J 10 9 8 7 5
```

Vulnerable: Both
Dealer: South

West	North	East	South
			2♣
Pass	2♠	Pass	3♣
Pass	3♦	Pass	5♣
Pass	6♣	Pass	Pass
Pass			

Opening lead: ♦3

Oswald Jacoby got back from the Pacific just in time to play in the 1945 Spingold. The Four Aces had broken up with his departure shortly after the start of the war, but he played with Ted Lightner as his partner and Howard Schenken and Sam Fry Jr. as the other half of the team.

Jacoby was pessimistic. He felt that his four-year absence from bridge would not be conducive to successful play. Howard and Sam weren't confident either, but Ted, usually the least optimistic of bridge players, said, "No one is going to beat us."

They didn't either. Here is Ted at work against Charles Goren and the late Sidney Silodor in the semi-final match.

Jacoby's six-club call was optimistic to say the least, but after three years in the war zone he can be excused for overbidding.

The play was fast and simple. Ted cashed a high heart at trick two, ruffed a heart, led dummy's last club, hopped up with the king and showed his hand when the queen dropped.

If any of you readers think that Ted was lucky, you are right. But he had also made the correct play. Normally the correct play is to lead twice from dummy and to play the jack, but this time there was no way to lead twice from dummy and Ted's play of the king gave him a better chance for the loss of only one club.

Lady luck saves declarer

```
                NORTH
                ♠ 7 5
                ♥ A 6
                ♦ Q 7 3
                ♣ A Q J 10 9 6
WEST                      EAST
♠ - - - -                 ♠ Q J 10 9 8 4 3
♥ Q J 10 9 8 5 3 2        ♥ 7
♦ 6                       ♦ J 8 5 2
♣ 7 5 4 3                 ♣ K
                SOUTH
                ♠ A K 6 2
                ♥ K 4
                ♦ A K 10 9 4
                ♣ 8 2
```

Vulnerable: North-South
Dealer: East

West	North	East	South
		3♠	3 NT
4♥	5♥	Pass	5♠
Pass	7 NT	Pass	Pass
Pass			

Opening lead: ♥Q

The late Kenneth Konstam was one of England's greatest bridge players and was particularly effective in rubber bridge play.

His three-notrump call was optimistic as was his spade cue bid and he found himself in a grand slam contract.

The first three tricks went to king of hearts, king and queen of diamonds. West showed out and it was an easy matter to finesse against East's jack and run the rest of the suit. Then Konstam cashed the ace of spades just to see if West would follow. Needless to say, he didn't and now the complete count of everyone's distribution was available. West had been dealt eight hearts, one diamond and four clubs.

Konstam led a club toward dummy and went up with the ace to pick up West's singleton king and bring the grand slam home.

East was bitter and accused Konstam of having peeked in his hand.

The accusation had no merit. Konstam had learned that the clubs were going to split 4-1. Hence, there was no way to make his contract unless East's singleton club was the king. A slim chance is better than no chance at all, so Konstam had availed himself of the slim chance.

Finesse or squeeze?

```
              NORTH
              ♠ Q 9 6 4
              ♥ A J 2
              ♦ A 8 2
              ♣ Q 5 4

WEST                    EAST
♠ 8 7                   ♠ 5
♥ Q 8 7 4 3             ♥ 10 9 6
♦ 7 5                   ♦ K Q 10 9 4 3
♣ J 9 8 6               ♣ 10 7 2

              SOUTH
              ♠ A K J 10 3 2
              ♥ K 5
              ♦ J 6
              ♣ A K 3
```

Vulnerable: North-South
Dealer: North

West	North	East	South
	1♣	2♦	2♠
Pass	3♠	Pass	4 NT
Pass	5♥	Pass	5 NT
Pass	6♣	Pass	6♠
Pass	Pass	Pass	

Opening lead: ♦7

South starts with 12 top tricks at either no trump or spades and can score his 13th by a simple heart finesse or a squeeze against East.

We'll show you the potential squeeze first. East has made one of those weak jump overcalls in diamonds. South takes dummy's ace at trick one and if he now runs off all his clubs and trumps he comes down to a three card ending. Dummy holds his three hearts, declarer his two hearts and jack of diamonds. East must hold one high diamond and as a result if he started with three or more hearts, including the queen, he would have had to unguard it.

A rubber bridge player in a six contract would ignore the finesse and take his slam. You would think that a match point player who had stopped at six spades would do the same. Yet when Barry Crane, who is one of the best — if not the best — match point player in the world and certainly the most successful, risked his contract when he played this hand at six spades some years back.

Here is his explanation. "I considered bidding more, but finally decided not to. I tend to overbid, so it looked as if lots of declarers would be in six no trump and would refuse the finesse to play safe. I wanted to beat them and the overtrick actually gave me a good score. Furthermore, I felt that East's weak bid greatly increased the chance that West would hold the queen of hearts."

'Trump management'

```
            NORTH
            ♠ 10 9 8 5
            ♥ K 4
            ♦ A J 7 4
            ♣ J 7 3
WEST                    EAST
♠ K 4                   ♠ 7 6 2
♥ 9 7 3                 ♥ A J 10 5
♦ 10 8 6 3             ♦ 9 5 2
♣ Q 9 8 2             ♣ K 10 4
            SOUTH
            ♠ A Q J 3
            ♥ Q 8 6 2
            ♦ K Q
            ♣ A 6 5
```

Vulnerable: North-South
Dealer: South

West	North	East	South
			1 NT
Pass	2♣	Pass	2♠
Pass	4♠	Pass	Pass
Pass			

Opening lead: ♣2

Here is a hand played by the late Albert H. Morehead, who for many years was Culbertson's right hand man. He reached four spades after a Stayman response to his opening notrump.

Against any lead but a club the hand would be a cinch. But he got a club lead.

He elected to play low from dummy and East stuck in the 10 to force Al's ace. He needed a club discard right away so he played the king and then queen of diamonds, overtaking the queen in order to get one club discard on the jack.

Now he had one club loser, one sure heart loser, one possible trump loser and two more possible heart losers. It was easy for Albert to see that as long as he could prevent three trump leads he could get to ruff two hearts with dummy's trumps and even if one heart got over-ruffed he would be home with 10 tricks.

Therefore, he led dummy's king of hearts. East took his ace and led back a trump, but now Al could afford to finesse. West took his king and led a second trump, but declarer was in full control. He won, cashed the heart queen, ruffed a heart, ruffed the last diamond and ruffed his last low heart.

The defense still scored the last trick, but that was only their third.

Imaginative ways of yore

```
              NORTH
              ♠ A 9
              ♥ K Q 10 5 4
              ♦ A 10 8 6 5
              ♣ K
WEST                  EAST
♠ K Q J 10 8 7        ♠ 6 4 3 2
♥ 9 2                 ♥ 8 3
♦ Q 7 4 2             ♦ J
♣ 3                   ♣ Q 10 7 6 4 2
              SOUTH
              ♠ 5
              ♥ A J 7 6
              ♦ K 9 3
              ♣ A J 9 8 5
```

Vulnerable: Both
Dealer: South

West	North	East	South
			1♣
1♠	2♦	Pass	3♥
Pass	7♥	Pass	Pass
Pass			

Opening lead: ♠ K

Sam Fry (life master number 10) was Sam Fry Jr. back in 1931. His partner the late Edward Hymes Jr., became life master number 23.

Their bidding of today's hand is indicative of how experts had to use imagination back in 1932.

Sam's opening club bid was normal and sound then as it is now. West might have made a weak jump overcall, but that bid was invented by 28-year-old Oswald Jacoby some six months later.

Hymes could not force with two hearts. He would have had to jump to three to force, so he elected to cue bid two spades. Sam should probably have bid just three clubs. But even at 69 (his current age) Sam is a most aggressive bidder, so he tried three hearts.

Eddie, who always looked for something brilliant, decided that seven hearts would be the most brilliant bid at his disposal. He bid it.

Sam didn't think it was brilliant when he saw the dummy and realized that it would take a lot of luck to bring home all the tricks.

He won the spade, cashed dummy's king of clubs, drew trumps with two leads and cashed his ace of clubs in the hope that something really good would happen in that suit. But West showed out.

Now he needed real luck in diamonds. He cashed his king, noted the fall of the jack from East, finessed against the queen and everything had come up roses.

Fast play, quick reward

```
            NORTH
          ♠ Q J 10 7
          ♥ 10 4
          ♦ 10 8 6 5
          ♣ 6 5 3
WEST                EAST
♠ K                 ♠ 5 4 2
♥ A K Q 9 8 6       ♥ 7 3 2
♦ Q 7 3 2           ♦ J 9 4
♣ A 4               ♣ 9 8 7 2
            SOUTH
          ♠ A 9 8 6 3
          ♥ J 5
          ♦ A K
          ♣ K Q J 10
```

Vulnerable: Neither
Dealer: South

West	North	East	South
			1♠
2♥	Pass	Pass	3♣
4♥	4♠	Pass	Pass
Pass			

Opening lead:♥K

West was the late Mike Gottlieb, one of the all-time great players and noted for his brilliant defense.

South was the late Charles Lochridge. Charley was not quite the player Mike was, but his many triumphs included the 1937 and 1939 Vanderbilt cups. His forte was quick but exceptionally good dummy play.

The play at four spades was really fast.

Mike opened the king of hearts and continued with the ace and queen after East played the deuce and then the trey.

Charley ruffed with dummy's 10 and led the queen without a moment's hesitation. East followed small and Charley went up with his ace and dropped Mike's king. He conceded a trick to the ace of clubs and scored his game.

"Well-played, as always," said Mike. "You're too tough for me."

"A cinch," said Charley. "You found the only way to get me to dummy. Obviously, you wanted me there."

The whole play is not too unusual. It pays declarer to beware when an expert gives him a present. The interesting feature is that these two made all their plays instantaneously. We don't know why Mike didn't lead ace and another club and hope to get a trick in diamonds, but the real credit goes to Charley who knew instantaneously what Mike was doing.

Inviting defense to err

```
            NORTH
          ♠ A Q 10 9 5 3
          ♥ A Q J 2
          ♦ 4
          ♣ 7 5
WEST              EAST
♠ 7              ♠ K 2
♥ 6 4 3          ♥ K 10 9 7
♦ Q 9 3          ♦ A K 10 8 7 5
♣ K J 10 8 3 2   ♣ Q
            SOUTH
          ♠ J 8 6 4
          ♥ 8 5
          ♦ J 6 2
          ♣ A 9 6 4
```

Vulnerable: North-South
Dealer: East

West	North	East	South
		1♦	Pass
2♣	Dbl.	2♦	2♠
Pass	4♠	Pass	Pass
Pass			

Opening lead: ♦ 3

Here is a hand that shows the late John Crawford, one of the greatest players of all time, in action.

East won the first trick with the king of diamonds and shifted to the queen of clubs. John was looking at one loser in each suit unless he could drop a singleton king. East was marked with both major-suit kings for his opening bid.

John worked out a line of play that would give East a chance to make a mistake and let him make his contract.

He took his ace of clubs immediately, ruffed his six of diamonds and played ace and a small spade. East was in with the king and wasted no time thinking. He cashed his ace of diamonds!

East assumed that John would ruff in dummy, but East was wrong. John discarded dummy's last club.

East had gotten himself caught in an end play at trick six.

If he led a heart he would take care of John's heart loser for him, so East led a fourth diamond. This allowed John to discard a heart and take a ruffing finesse against East's king to get his 10 tricks.

If East had stopped to think he could have led a low diamond instead of the ace, but all defenders are not perfect and East had gone wrong.

A once and always master

```
              NORTH
              ♠ J 9 3 2
              ♥ A 6
              ♦ A 9 6 3
              ♣ 8 4 2
WEST                    EAST
♠ 8 7                   ♠ Q 10
♥ Q J 7 2               ♥ 10 3
♦ 10 8 4                ♦ J 7 5 2
♣ K Q J 5               ♣ 10 9 7 6 3
              SOUTH
              ♠ A K 6 5 4
              ♥ K 9 8 5 4
              ♦ K Q
              ♣ A
```

Vulnerable: Both
Dealer: South

West	North	East	South
			2♠
Pass	3♠	Pass	4 NT
Pass	5 NT	Pass	7♠
Pass	Pass	Pass	

Opening lead: ♣K

In 1932, that bridge genius Ely Culbertson conceived the idea of using the four-notrump bid to find out about aces and the king of genuinely bid suits.

The convention had two weaknesses. 1)It was extremely complicated. 2)The four notrump bidder needed to hold either three aces or two aces and the king of a bid suit in order to bid four notrump.

North and South had no trouble getting to seven with this convention. Of course, South did not know how good North's trumps were. He did know he had the missing two aces since the five-notrump bid had shown this.

As you can see, the seven bid is a spade lay down. All declarer has to do is to play his ace and king of trumps and claim.

Unfortunately for South, a 1933 expert, the great Ely was defending against the grand slam reached by his disciples.

When South led his ace of spades at trick two Ely, who sat East, dropped the queen.

Now declarer abandoned the idea of leading a second trump and went after hearts with every intention of ruffing two of them in dummy. It didn't work. Ely overruffed with his 10 and the cinch grand slam had gone to Davy Jones' locker.

Stellar British play

```
                NORTH
              ♠ A K 6
              ♥ 5
              ♦ A Q J 10 8 4
              ♣ A 8 3
WEST                      EAST
♠ 5 4 3                   ♠ J
♥ A Q 10 4 2              ♥ 6 3
♦ - - - -                 ♦ 9 7 6 5 3 2
♣ J 10 9 7 5              ♣ K Q 4 2
                SOUTH
              ♠ Q 10 9 8 7 2
              ♥ K J 9 8 7
              ♦ K
              ♣ 6
```

Vulnerable: North-South
Dealer: North

West	North	East	South
	1♦	Pass	1♠
Dbl.	Redbl.	2♣	3♠
4♣	4 NT	Pass	5♣
Pass	6♦	Pass	Pass
Pass			

Opening lead: ♣J

John Collings of Great Britain has long been known as one of the greatest dummy players of all-time. In today's hand we see him in six spades against the Hungarians. John won the first trick with dummy's ace of clubs, cashed the ace of spades and was happy to see both opponents following. Then he stopped to review all the bidding and finally led dummy's singleton heart to his king and East's ace. It didn't matter what East did now. John was sure to be able to ruff a heart in dummy, draw trumps and wind up with his six trumps, one heart ruff, four diamonds and the ace of clubs.

We do not know the bidding at the other table, but the same six spade contract was reached and the same jack of clubs opened.

The play for the first two tricks was the same, but at trick three the declarer played a second trump and then tried to cash his king of diamonds. West ruffed and cashed his ace of hearts.

We sympathize with the Hungarian South, but must give real credit to John Collings. He had guarded against a 6-0 diamond break.

Invention of a convention

```
            NORTH
            ♠ Q 8 7
            ♥ A Q J 9 8
            ♦ K Q
            ♣ J 10 2
WEST                 EAST
♠ 6 4 2              ♠ 5 3
♥ 10 3               ♥ 7 5 2
♦ J 10 9 5           ♦ A 8 6 4 3 2
♣ A 6 4 3            ♣ K Q
            SOUTH
            ♠ A K J 10 9
            ♥ K 6 4
            ♦ 7
            ♣ 9 8 7 5
```

Vulnerable: Neither
Dealer: North

West	North	East	South
	1♥	Pass	1♠
Pass	2♣	Pass	4♠
Pass	Pass	Pass	

Opening lead: ♦ J

This hand shows the invention of a common sense convention. The late Sonny Moyse (long editor of the Bridge World) sat West. The late Al Morehead (once editor of the Bridge World, but best known as bridge editor of the New York Times) sat East.

Moyse and Morehead claimed to be bad card holders and they certainly were with today's hand.

Three notrump is unbeatable. But back in 1930, and right now in 1979, any North-South pair would arrive at the four-spade contract.

Al won the diamond lead with his ace. A club shift was obvious and Al made the abnormal lead of the queen rather than the normal king lead.

When he continued with the king, Sonny went into communion with nature. Why had Al led the queen?

Finally, Sonny said to himself, "He must be meaning to tell me something and that something must be that he was dealt just those two clubs."

So Sonny rose with his ace, gave his partner a club ruff and still was minus 50 points since lucky South had 100 honors.

'The great unblock'

```
                NORTH
             ♠ A Q 2
             ♥ A K Q J
             ♦ Q J 10 9 8 7
             ♣ - - - -
WEST                    EAST
♠ K J 10 9 8 7        ♠ 6 5 4 3
♥ 5 4 3 2             ♥ - - - -
♦ - - - -            ♦ 6 5 4 3 2
♣ K Q J              ♣ 5 4 3 2
                SOUTH
             ♠ - - - -
             ♥ 10 9 8 7 6
             ♦ A K
             ♣ A 10 9 8 7 6
```

Vulnerable: Both
Dealer: West

West	North	East	South
3♠	Dbl.	Pass	4♣
Pass	5♣	Pass	6♣
Pass	6♦	Pass	6♥
Pass	7♥	Pass	Pass
Pass			

Opening lead: ♣K

Here is a hand that has been around in one form or another since time immemorable by bridge standards.

The late Geoffrey Mott-Smith called it "The great unblock." In today's format as presented by Easley Blackwood in the American Contract Bridge League bulletin a lot of red herrings have been drawn against the problem solver's path.

Can he set up clubs? Can he do something with that ace-queen of spades against West's king?, etc. Should he ruff in dummy?, etc.

The answer is that South should discard a diamond from dummy and win with his ace. Then he leads a trump to dummy and ruffs the deuce of spades. He leads a second trump and ruffs the queen of spades. He has one trump left so he leads it to dummy. Now the king of diamonds is discarded on the ace of trumps and the ace of diamonds on the ace of spades. The great unblock has been accomplished and dummy's diamonds are good.

In his introduction of the hand Easley wonders if maybe our grandparents saw this in whist problems. We feel that Geoffrey probably concocted it about 50 years ago when he, Easley Blackwood and Oswald Jacoby still had parents and maybe grandparents alive.

Incidentally, Easley didn't dare to show bidding. We have made it up to the best of our ability.

Use half an end play

```
              NORTH
              ♠ Q J
              ♥ K 10 6 3
              ♦ K J 7
              ♣ A K 5 3
WEST                      EAST
♠ K 10 8 7 5 3           ♠ 6 2
♥ 7 2                    ♥ A 4
♦ A 9                    ♦ 10 8 6 4 2
♣ J 9 4                  ♣ Q 10 7 6
              SOUTH
              ♠ A 9 4
              ♥ Q J 9 8 5
              ♦ Q 5 3
              ♣ 8 2
```

Vulnerable: Neither
Dealer: North

West	North	East	South
	1♣	Pass	1♥
Pass	3♥	Pass	4♥
Pass	Pass	Pass	

Opening lead: ♦A

Albert Dormer is best known as a writer, but in 1952 when he was just a young bridge player, he played a most instructive hand.

Derek Rimington describes it with the comment, "Half an end play is better than no end play at all."

West opened the ace of diamonds against Albert's four heart contract and continued with the nine in spite of getting the discouraging deuce from his partner. It was obvious to Albert that West wanted a diamond ruff and that if East held the heart ace there would be no way to prevent it.

No loser-on-loser play was available, but Albert found that half an end play.

He cashed dummy's ace and king of clubs and ruffed a club. Now he led a trump. East took his ace and gave his partner that desired diamond ruff, but the half end play had developed.

West had been dealt six spades, two hearts, two diamonds and three clubs so he was left with nothing but spades and had to lead away from his king.

Note that East could have led a spade to spoil the end play, but in that case there would be no diamond ruff.

A simple convention

```
                NORTH
                ♠ A K J 6 3 2
                ♥ A K 7 5 4
                ♦ 5 3
                ♣ - - - -

WEST                        EAST
♠ Q 9                       ♠ 10 8 4
♥ 8 6                       ♥ 3
♦ K Q 10 7 2                ♦ A J 8 6
♣ J 9 7 3                   ♣ 10 6 5 4 2

                SOUTH
                ♠ 7 5
                ♥ Q J 10 9 2
                ♦ 9 4
                ♣ A K Q 8
```

Vulnerable: Both
Dealer: North

West	North	East	South
	1♠	Pass	2♥
Pass	5♦	Pass	5♥
Pass	Pass	Pass	

Opening lead: ♦K

Bill Root and Dick Pavlicek are two of the nicest people in bridge or in anything else. Thus, they give the late Albert Morehead credit for this simple artificial convention. The jump to five of an unbid suit when you are in an uncontested auction asks partner to show first- or second-round control or no control as the case may be.

Bill and Dick are too modest. They deserve most of the credit for this. It is simple although the chance to use it occurs so seldom that any ordinary player is likely to forget it before he gets a chance to use it. Let's see it at work.

North might well open with a forcing bid, but he elects to bid just one spade. South makes a normal two-heart response.

North looks at his hand and sees that he wants to be in seven if South has first-round diamond control, in six if South has second-round diamond control and just in five if South can't take either the first or second diamond lead.

South looks at his two little diamonds and makes the cheapest bid he can to show that. It happens to be five hearts. If South held a singleton diamond or the king he would bid five spades while with first-round diamond control he would go one more step and bid five notrump.

A beautiful convention for anyone who will remember it.

On taking your best shot

```
                NORTH
                ♠ 7 6 3
                ♥ A 2
                ♦ 8 6 5 4
                ♣ A 7 4 3
WEST                      EAST
♠ A J                     ♠ 9 8 5
♥ 10 7 5 4                ♥ J 9 8 3
♦ K Q 10 9                ♦ J 7 3
♣ J 8 2                   ♣ Q 10 6
                SOUTH
                ♠ K Q 10 4 2
                ♥ K Q 6
                ♦ A 2
                ♣ K 9 5
```

Vulnerable: Both
Dealer: South

West	North	East	South
			1♠
Pass	2♠	Pass	4♠
Pass	Pass	Pass	

Opening lead: ♦ K

Mike Gottlieb, one of the greatest players of the Thirties who had already won three Vanderbilt cups before he retired in 1936, has started playing bridge again in California. He recently played in a sectional Swiss team in Palo Alto where his team won with a score of eight wins out of eight matches.

Here is a hand he played against Ely Culbertson back in 1933. The play was short and effective. Mike won the diamond lead, entered dummy with the ace of hearts and led a spade to his king. Culbertson won with the ace and played two more diamonds.

Mike ruffed, went to dummy with the ace of clubs, led a second trump, rose with his queen, dropped Ely's jack and while he still had to lose a club he had his game home.

Why did Mike play for that jack drop?

He explained later that in similar circumstances, Ely always ducked with ace-small. Hence, when Ely won the first spade with the ace and East followed low on the second spade, Ely either had held ace-jack doubleton, ace-jack-small or singleton ace. As there was no way to avoid the loss of another spade trick against the last two, Mike utilized his only chance.

Amazing defense wins

```
                NORTH
              ♠ K 9 4 2
              ♥ K J 9 3
              ♦ 10 6 5
              ♣ Q 3
WEST                      EAST
♠ Q J 8 6 5               ♠ 10 7
♥ 7 6 2                   ♥ Q 8 5
♦ 8 4                     ♦ K Q 9 7 2
♣ J 9 4                   ♣ A 10 8
                SOUTH
              ♠ A 3
              ♥ A 10 4
              ♦ A J 3
              ♣ K 7 6 5 2
```

Vulnerable: Both
Dealer: South

West	North	East	South
			1 NT
Pass	2♦	Dbl.	Pass
Pass	2 NT	Pass	3 NT
Pass	Pass	Pass	

Opening lead: ♦8

In today's hand we see Rob Sheehan of the British team putting up an amazingly brilliant defense to beat a three no-trump contract by Poland.

The Polish pair were playing two-way Stayman so North's two diamond response asked for majors and forced to game. Sheehan doubled for a diamond lead so that West opened the eight of diamonds against South's three no-trump.

Rob started his defense by playing the diamond nine. South was in with the jack and led a club to dummy's queen. Sheehan played the eight!

At this stage of the proceedings South could have made six if he had known what Sheehan was up to. All he had to do would be to lead dummy's last club and rise with his king, then drop the ace and jack together and finally guess the heart position. But South was only human. He did lead the club, but played low after East played the 10. West took his jack and led the four of diamonds.

Rob's queen forced declarer's ace and a third club was led. Now East produced the ace and cashed his last three diamonds to set a contract that made easily when Great Britain held the North and South hands.

Hands About Actual People

Great American save

```
              NORTH
              ♠ 10 3
              ♥ 9 7 3
              ♦ Q 8 7 6 3 2
              ♣ Q 8
WEST                      EAST
♠ A K                     ♠ Q 7 6 4
♥ A Q                     ♥ K J 10 6 2
♦ J 9                     ♦ A 10 5
♣ A K 10 9 6 4 2          ♣ 7
              SOUTH
              ♠ J 9 8 5 2
              ♥ 8 5 4
              ♦ K 4
              ♣ J 5 3
```

Vulnerable: North-South
Dealer: West

West	North	East	South
2♣	Pass	2♥	Pass
3♣	Pass	3♥	Pass
4♥	Pass	5♦	Pass
5♣	Pass	7♥	7♠
Pass	Pass	Dbl.	Pass
Pass	Pass		

Opening lead: ♣K

The bidding in the box is what took place when Jeff Meckstroth held the South cards in the world championship match. Munir and Fazli of Pakistan had bid a vulnerable seven hearts. Jeff looked at his three small hearts and three clubs to the jack and was certain they would make it for a score of plus 2,210. Down 11 at seven spades would only cost him 2,100 and he might get out for less. In any event, he did bid seven spades. Actually, he got a good dummy for his purposes. Perfect defense would have set him 10 tricks, but he got out for down nine and minus just 1,700 for a net gain of 10 IMPs because Solodar and Arnold in the other room bid and made the grand slam.

Meckstroth's bid reminds Oswald Jacoby that when the Whist Club of New York and the Portland Club of London were contract's law-making body, he, Ely Culbertson and the other American experts were asked to advise.

He suggested the present penalties to replace far larger ones in use at that time.

The first response was that people would take all sorts of absurd saves against slam bids, but when Ely Culbertson came to Jacoby's support the current penalties were accepted.

It has made little difference. In fact, this brilliant save by Meckstroth is about the first time we have seen it in top competition.

A remarkable end play

```
                NORTH
                ♠ A K
                ♥ Q 4 3
                ♦ K Q 10 8 7 6
                ♣ 9 2
WEST                      EAST
♠ J 7 2                   ♠ Q 6 5 4
♥ J 10 9 5                ♥ 6
♦ 9 4                     ♦ J 5 3
♣ A 10 8 6                ♣ Q J 7 5 4
                SOUTH
                ♠ 10 9 8 3
                ♥ A K 8 7 2
                ♦ A 2
                ♣ K 3
```

Vulnerable: East-West
Dealer: East

West	North	East	South
		Pass	1♥
Pass	2♦	Pass	2 NT
Pass	3♣	Pass	4♦
Pass	4♥	Pass	4 NT
Pass	5♦	Pass	6♥
Dbl.	Pass	Pass	6 NT
Pass	Pass	Pass	

Opening lead: ♥J

Most players in the Life Master Pairs stopped at four hearts and were happy when the bad trump break held them to five. A few bid to six and most went down one undoubled.

One West player could not stand prosperity. He doubled six hearts. South ran to six no trump. Now West wished he hadn't doubled six hearts. He passsed and had to lead something. The jack of hearts looked pretty safe and he placed it on the table.

It turned out to be a real mistake, while either a diamond or spade lead would have left declarer one trick short. The heart lead gave Harvard professor Richard Zeckhauser a chance to develop a remarkable end play.

Dick won the lead in his hand and led his eight of hearts. He planned to duck if West ducked, but West played his 10 spot.

Now Dick went after diamonds. The jack dropped so he cashed six diamonds and continued with dummy's ace and king of spades to come down to a three card ending. His three cards were king-seven of hearts and king of clubs. West had to blank his ace of clubs in order to keep a guard for his nine of hearts.

Dick led a club from dummy. West took his ace, but had to give declarer the last two tricks with his two hearts.

Law according to Adam

```
                NORTH
                ♠ 4
                ♥ K J
                ♦ A 5
                ♣ A J 9 8 7 6 5 4
WEST                    EAST
♠ 8 7 6 5 3 2           ♠ - - - -
♥ Q 10 5               ♥ 8 7 6 3
♦ - - - -             ♦ K J 10 9 8 7 6 3 2
♣ K Q 10 2             ♣ - - - -
                SOUTH
                ♠ A K Q J 10 9
                ♥ A 9 4 2
                ♦ Q 4
                ♣ 3
```

Vulnerable: North-South
Dealer: North

West	North	East	South
	1♣	4♦	4 NT
Pass	5♥	Pass	6♠
Pass	Pass	Pass	

Opening lead: ♣K

No collection would be complete unless it included one played by the late Adam Meredith. Adam was a law unto himself. He arrived at hopeless contracts on his own style of bidding only to pull a rabbit out of the hat and bring them home.

Not that we can blame him much for getting to six spades. He was allergic to pre-empts and after East's four diamond pre-empt Adam bid what to him had to be a conservative six spades.

He put dummy's ace of clubs on West's king. East chucked a diamond and Adam knew that East had been dealt 13 red cards. Thus, West was marked with six spades and Adam was going to have to play the hand in no-trump since he had to pull all of West's teeth.

Even then it was essential that East have exactly four hearts and nine diamonds and that West's three hearts include both queen and 10.

Now Adam was ready to operate. He ran off all six trumps and carefully discarded the ace of diamonds and four of clubs from dummy.

Now he led a heart to dummy's jack, cashed the king and led the five of diamonds. East took his king, but Adam made the last three tricks with the queen of diamonds and the ace-nine of hearts.

Unsound bid soundly made

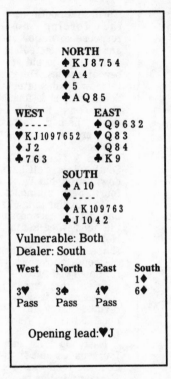

NORTH
♠ K J 8 7 5 4
♥ A 4
♦ 5
♣ A Q 8 5

WEST
♠ - - - -
♥ K J 10 9 7 6 5 2
♦ J 2
♣ 7 6 3

EAST
♠ Q 9 6 3 2
♥ Q 8 3
♦ Q 8 4
♣ K 9

SOUTH
♠ A 10
♥ - - - -
♦ A K 10 9 7 6 3
♣ J 10 4 2

Vulnerable: Both
Dealer: South

West	North	East	South
			1♦
3♥	3♠	4♥	6♦
Pass	Pass	Pass	

Opening lead: ♥J

Here is a hand played some years ago by Terence Reese, one of the greatest players of all time.

His jump to six diamonds was unsound, but he had a lot going for him. Maybe the bid would be a winner. Maybe East or West would take a phantom save at six hearts. Anyway he bid it.

When dummy came down he saw that he had a pretty good chance if trumps would just break 3-2. He ruffed the heart lead to leave the ace in dummy as a possible extra entry. Then he cashed his ace and king of trumps and ace of spades. West showed out, but Reese still had a pretty good shot at the slam. All that was required was to find East with the queen of trumps. So, Terrence led his 10 of spades to dummy's king and returned the jack. East could do no better than cover with the queen and Terence ruffed. Then he threw East in with a diamond.

East had to lead a heart. South discarded a club on dummy's ace and led the eight of spades to establish the last two spades for two more club discards and his slam.

Of course, if West had opened a club the slam would have failed, but West was only human.

Freak hand, odd result

```
              NORTH
              ♠ J 2
              ♥ - - - -
              ♦ 9 8 6 3 2
              ♣ A K 10 8 6 5
WEST                    EAST
♠ Q 9 7 6 4             ♠ A K 10 8 5 3
♥ 6                     ♥ K J 10 8 2
♦ K 10 5 4             ♦ - - - -
♣ J 9 4                 ♣ Q 2
              SOUTH
              ♠ - - - -
              ♥ A Q 9 7 5 4 3
              ♦ A Q J 7
              ♣ 7 3
```

Vulnerable: North-South
Dealer: South

West	North	East	South
			1♥
Pass	1 NT	Pass	4♥
Pass	Pass	Dbl.	Pass
Pass	Pass		

Opening lead: ♦ 4

Here is one of those freak hands that was actually dealt in a friendly IMP match where five of the eight players were former world champions.

The bidding in the box took place at a table where North, South and East were among the five champions.

North and South were using the forcing no-trump response to major openings and East elected to pass rather than to bid any number of spades. He expected to show spades later on, but South jumped to four hearts. East could hardly believe the bid he had heard, but he recovered from his shock to double.

Had West opened a spade South might well have gone down three, but West led his fourth-best diamond. East ruffed, led his king of spades and got his second shock of the hand when South ruffed. Not that South was in good shape. He had to lose one diamond and four trumps for down just two.

As is the case with all freakish hands with rather divided strength, plus-500 doesn't have to be a really good score.

East and West can make four spades and if they get doubled their score is 590. However, in this match it led to a real swing.

At the other table Bob Hamman and Bob Wolff were North and South. Bob, we don't know which one, played in five diamonds doubled. We don't know how he made it except that he did for a plus of 750 and a net gain of 15 IMPs.

As Simon says

```
                    NORTH
                    ♠ J 7 3 2
                    ♥ K 5 4
                    ♦ Q 2
                    ♣ A 8 6 3
WEST                            EAST
♠ Q 10 8 6                      ♠ - - - -
♥ J 9                           ♥ Q 10 8 6 3
♦ 10 5 3                        ♦ J 8 7 4
♣ K Q J 7                       ♣ 10 9 4 2
                    SOUTH
                    ♠ A K 9 5 4
                    ♥ A 7 2
                    ♦ A K 9 6
                    ♣ 5
```

Vulnerable: North-South
Dealer: East

West	North	East	South
		Pass	2♠
Pass	3♠	Pass	4 NT
Pass	5♦	Pass	6♠
Pass	Pass	Pass	

Opening lead: ♣K

John E. Simon of St. Louis is a bridge aficionado. Born in 1897, Jack still heads the oldest stock exchange firm west of the Mississippi. He plays lots of rubber bridge but has given up tournament play.

The really remarkable feature about his three national wins is that they all were in tough men's team events and occurred in 1965, 1972 and 1973.

Jack is an overbidder at rubber bridge. In so doing he keeps lots of pressure on his opponents. Furthermore, he has a faculty of playing to make doubtful contracts.

Most players would go down at six spades, due to the 4-0 trump break. Here is how Jack made the slam:

He took dummy's ace of clubs and ruffed a club at trick two. Then he led his ace of spades and got the bad news. Undaunted he led a diamond to dummy's queen and ruffed another club.

Then came a heart to the king and a ruff of dummy's last club. Now he cashed his ace of hearts and ace-king of diamonds while West had to follow suit. Now he led a red card.

West was down to Q-10-8 of trumps but could only score one trick with them. Jack still held his trump king and dummy the J-7-3, so it made no difference what card West ruffed with. He could only score his queen.

Bridge among the veterans

```
                NORTH
                ♠ Q 7
                ♥ 9 5 3
                ♦ A 8 4 2
                ♣ A 9 7 6
WEST                        EAST
♠ K J 10                    ♠ 9 5 2
♥ J 7 4                     ♥ A Q 6 2
♦ Q 10 7 3                  ♦ 9 6 5
♣ Q 8 2                     ♣ J 5 4
                SOUTH
                ♠ A 8 6 4 3
                ♥ K 10 8
                ♦ K J
                ♣ K 10 3
```

Vulnerable: East-West
Dealer: South

West	North	East	South
			1 NT
Pass	3 NT	Pass	Pass
Pass			

Opening lead: ♦ 3

No list of 80-year-old players would be complete without a hand played by the late Jack Ehrlenbach. Jack was the first life master on the Pacific Coast.

He only won one national, the 1949 mixed teams. His partner was bridge teacher Helen Cale. The other half of the team was Mr. and Mrs. Arnold Kauder. Mary Jane Kauder is now Mary Jane Farell and is one of the top women players of all time.

Jack was only 65 when he won that national, and he continued to play with pupils until his death at an age well past 80.

Jack usually played with rather poor players and really tried to make sure that he got to play doubtful no-trump contracts. Here we see Jack with a 14 point no-trump. Officially, Jack used standard no-trumps so North raised him right to game.

The diamond lead came to his jack. He led a spade toward dummy. West rose with the king and led the four of hearts to his partner's ace. A heart was returned. Jack took his king, led a spade to dummy's queen, came back to his hand with the king of diamonds and was home when spades broke 3-3.

Three no-trump bid and made would have been a near top, but Jack came home with 11 tricks. East and West each let one club go. So Jack wound up with four spades, one heart and three tricks in each minor suit.